IRONY
EVIDENCE FOR GOD

NICK WHITE

Copyright © 2017 Nick White

All rights reserved

ISBN: 1542372569

ISBN-13: 978-1542372565

To my family and friends

CONTENTS

Introduction		*5*
Chapter 1	*The Irony of Fate*	*10*
Chapter 2	*Irony in My Life*	*22*
Chapter 3	*Irony in Names*	*39*
Chapter 4	*Isn't it Ironic?*	*42*
Chapter 5	*A Demon Named Irony*	*50*
Chapter 6	*Irony in the Devil's Life*	*56*
Chapter 7	*Irony in God's Life*	*65*
Chapter 8	*The Law of Irony*	*78*
Chapter 9	*The Creation of Irony*	*85*
Chapter 10	*Who's to Blame?*	*98*
Chapter 11	*Irony as Evidence for God*	*109*
Chapter 12	*Irony in Your Life*	*119*
Conclusion		*122*

Introduction

'Irony is wasted on the stupid.'

Oscar Wilde

Irony itself would have you not read this book. It would cause everything to conspire to keep you from reading this book in the same way as it has made everything conspire to keep me from writing it.

Irony can be like a sharp sword which cuts away the superficial, seeming to separate the wheat from the chaff. And if God is brought into the equation, all kinds of strange things can happen.

Some people say that the first lesson of true wisdom is to understand that we are all fools. In the same way, although it may seem like insanity to claim that irony is evidence for God, the first lesson of sanity is that we are all mad (present company excluded). So please indulge the insanity. If only because irony and God can drive an otherwise sane person out of their mind.

Paradoxes aside, writing this book is a simple act of folly. You will not find many books which bring forward irony as credible evidence for God. Maybe they never get written. Maybe they get laughed into oblivion.

Although we are said to live in post-ironic and post-truth times, both irony and truth are still alive and kicking. The fact that we live in an age in which irony is unnoticed, sidelined and misunderstood does not mean that irony is dead. It is still used within all kinds of culture – from pop culture through to the high arts. From soap operas through to literary fiction. Irony in the hands of creators is still a sly nod to the intelligent. It is still the shape within the cloud, tree or rock face which some see and some do not.

Artists and writers will draw inspiration from the ironies they experience. Irony in life is called the irony of fate. But what is the source of this everyday irony? Is it meaningless? Is it simply a survival mechanism, the natural observation of patterns within a life story? Or is there anything more to it? Is it supposed to teach us something?

There can be a schadenfreude in seeing irony play out in other people's lives. But when we see that same Damocles sword hanging over our own heads the pleasure usually fades. Sometimes we don't even see the sword. And there seem to be few good ironies. In life, when the ironies we experience seem to have no creator, they are usually bitter and cruel.

Writing a half-accessible book about irony is as hard a task as reading about it. It is like trying to put wind into a jar, or to pin fire to a butterfly sample board. There will be feverish similes. There will be gobbledegook. There will be rambling and ranting.

Inevitably, any person attempting to analyse or pin down irony is going to fail or go mad. This is the nature of irony – it is such a powerful force that it will make fools of anyone who even attempts to analyse it. Catch a butterfly and pin it to a sample board and the beauty is lost in the end. The colours fade. The life is gone. Some people will say that the colours were never there in the first place. That the bright colours and patterns on the wings of the butterflies were imagined. And even if they see dim patterns on the fragile wings they say such patterns are meaningless and random, signifying nothing.

This book is written mainly for agnostics and for anyone who has noticed irony in their life. Believers may find it too critical of God. Atheists may find it too illogical. I only agree with atheists that the burden of proof is on the believer. This is written for agnostics, for those who instinctively blame God when something goes wrong. If any readers firmly don't believe in God then I don't think I'm going to be able to persuade them otherwise. I will only persuade them to laugh. And I admit, the idea that irony is evidence for God is laughable at first – you will find a million and one holes in my theory, a hundred thousand illogical assertions, strawmen and cognitive biases. My hope is that after laughing, some people will think about it. I have not written this book from a left brain, logical perspective (that much, I'm sure will be apparent). It is written from intuition, from the imagination. The imagination is the only way to study irony, it is the only effective hermeneutic. And so this is not so much a call to reason, as a call to imagination. A call to story. Because irony needs there to be a story.

I have tried my best to make this book as accessible as possible, but I have come to it from the position of a layman and not as an academic or theologian. I am approaching the subject as a writer, not as an intellectual. I will also attempt to be as pragmatic as possible – after all, what is the point of reading a book if it doesn't do you any good? But this is not a self-help book – it is an obscure book, from an obscure writer living in an obscure place. But perhaps the Ironist would have it that the obscure, the foolish and the mad would attempt to shame the wise.

A further irony has been that so many events seem to have conspired to keep me away from writing this. It was as if the universe didn't want me to write it. And perhaps I should have listened. Life events, work commitments and many responsibilities have prevented me from giving it attention. But I am stubborn and that is why you are reading these words (although ironically, even this sentence was interrupted).

I know, I know, 'That's not irony, that's just bad luck' I hear you think. But I would like to extend the definition of irony. Please indulge me in that. Whether any of it makes sense or not I will leave to your own decision and conscience. I have no intention of brow-beating you into holding any of the views I introduce. All I ask is that you think about it all.

Maybe books like this do get written but the author dies in an ironic way before they can be published. Irony acts as a trap. As a weapon which cuts and stings. Some people see that sword. And some do not. There are plenty of books about how scripture or nature are evidence for the existence of God. There are shelves full of attempts to present evidence for God (and against him). But there are no books about irony as evidence for God that I know of. So, at least, if you find the following illogical or insane, you will admit that this book is original.

I will be using a literary and narrative analysis of life alongside what remains of my common sense. I will be looking at people's lives in terms of story and looking at the meta-narrative of history and scripture in order to bring forward some half-credible evidence that the presence of irony points towards a creator or Ironist. There will be no abstract or methodology – research will be subjective. References will be the ones that most people are familiar with. Conclusions will be as pragmatic as possible.

Above all I am coming to this subject as a believer. I'm writing this book simply because my faith is sustained by observing the irony of fate. Apart from creation itself, I find that irony is the most persuasive argument for the existence of God. Hence this strange, obscure book. And irony is a personal life experience for all of us, whether we see the patterns or not.

Chapter 1 – The Irony of Fate

Jesus told them, "It is not the healthy who need a doctor, but the sick. I have not come to call the righteous, but sinners."'

Mark 2:17

To begin, I need to define my terms and for that I would like to refer to pop culture. Firstly, there is the obvious reference of Alanis Morissette's iconic song *'Ironic'*.

I can almost see you shaking your head already. Famous comedians have said that the things Alanis Morissette talks about are neither ironic nor suggestive of any intelligent ironist. Please be aware that I am likely to repeat her error in the examples of irony within this book. And as you shall see - that is the nature of irony for all of us.

What if the ultimate irony *'Ironic'* is that the song really is ironic and it's just that some people simply don't see that? Because the trouble with irony is that people often don't see it. It is like finding shapes in clouds. One person sees a face, the other person sees a cloud. And even if Alanis's examples don't amount to the strict definition of irony, they do align with Murphy's Law or Sod's Law. *'It's like rain on your wedding day'* implies something beyond bad luck. It implies that there's someone out to get you.

And so, I ask that you would indulge me as I play with and stretch the semantics a little. Basically, I'm calling for a redefinition of the word 'irony'. If you are determined to hold to the dictionary definition, then I may as well have called this book 'Crazily Bad Luck – Evidence for God' and my theory wouldn't entirely have changed. That's okay, but this whole book is going to be a case of 'The Emperors New Clothes' for you – with me saying the king is fully dressed and you saying the king is 'in the altogether'. In that story it is the adults who don't want to look silly for not seeing invisible clothes. And here, the onus is on me too. Somehow, I have to try to find evidence for invisible things. Things like irony.

The word 'irony' is defined in the dictionary in the following way:

irony[1]
ˈʌɪrəni/
noun
the expression of one's meaning by using language that normally signifies the opposite, typically for humorous or emphatic effect.

But in everyday life, when someone says, 'That's ironic', they rarely mean that someone has just said something opposite to a reality. In everyday life the definition is stretched.

The word is related to an ancient Greek character depicted in drama named 'Eiron'. Eiron was a sort of Socratic archetype who always won against his opponent (his nemesis being a proud bully named the 'Alazon'). The Eiron would always outwit the Alazon through a kind of feigned naivety. His questions would humiliate the Alazon and this was the pattern of many ancient plays. It is still the pattern for many modern day dramas such as *Columbo*. Okay, *Columbo* isn't modern – how about *New Tricks*. I know, I know, *New Tricks* is old too. I'm being ironic.

Take your favourite hero or heroine in fiction. Usually they will be using some form of Socratic irony to defeat their nemesis. Socratic irony is when a person asks a seemingly innocent question in order to win in a debate. It is the (relatively) humble character taking the proud character a peg or two down. It can happen both in fiction and real life.

But, when it comes to defining irony there is little consensus. There are even websites which ask whether people consider different things to be ironic or not. Few people agree. Some people strictly adhere to the idea that an irony must obey the dictionary definition. Others see irony in a looser manner. Ironic sensitivity is like a colour-blindness test – not everyone can see the patterns in the dots. Those who are not colour-blind will be able to spot the numbers easily. Those who are colour-blind will see no discernible pattern. It can be maddening for those who clearly see the pattern, attempting to show the colour-blind where the number is. (I am, incidentally (and perhaps, or perhaps not ironically), colour-blind.) Maybe irony is like a joke, which, once explained, loses its efficacy.

So what I'm calling for is a much looser definition of irony, and especially of the irony of fate. I'm proposing a much wider assessment of irony in everyday life simply because it is our experience and because language evolves. Specifically I would like to extend the definition of irony to include bad luck, hypocrisy and coincidence. Furthermore to stretch the definition of irony to truisms, synchronicity and paradox. I would like to do this because there are an army of people who also relate to irony in this looser sense. Language is subject to evolution – and as such it should encompass changing perspectives. When hordes of people see bad luck as ironic then maybe those who hold to the strict definition should relate to this new definition rather than pedantically assert that bad luck is not ironic.

Because bad luck really can seem ironic. In everyday understanding there sometimes really is a pattern in the cloud or the tree, in the events which occur. And, for those who understand this, there truly seems to be some kind of pernicious and malevolent power which seems to have got it in for us.

Most people understand their lives as narratives, as stories. Irony needs story. Psychotherapy works best when a person is understood in terms of story. It is a more holistic approach to dealing with health than the usual machine metaphor which most of the health profession seems to embrace. In the same way that stories have creators, the meta-narrative and history of the world can be said to have a creator. A kind of heavenly Storyteller. Because where there is a story there is usually a storyteller. And I would like to begin by suggesting that where there is irony, there is almost always an ironist.

In everyday speech we usually call these ironies of fate 'Sod's Law' or 'Murphy's Law', depending on whether we give a name to them and our outlook. These two laws differ slightly but I will go into that later.

So, to get to the point and quit my rambling, let's attempt to define irony again. Alanis would be proud of me.

Many thinking people will go beyond the logical dictionary definition when it comes to spotting irony in their own lives. It will depend on your personality and character on whether or not you are willing to accept this looser definition. Irony is not only found in the cruel Judge named 'Mr Goodwill'. Or the dentist named 'Mr Gentle' (his appointments always being at 2:30). Irony is found in Sod's Law, in the person you least want to see being in the place you least want to see them at the worst possible time. In the car jam when you are on the way to an interview. Or a thousand and other seemingly impossible situations which cause men and women to exclaim, 'What are the chances of that!?' These kind of things are bad luck, but when experienced subjectively, they seem to be ironic. They seem to be contrived. What I'm trying to suggest is that they are often not only bad luck – there really is something behind these things. Both someone and something signified by them.

Major ironies are often found in names and careers. Most people take truisms to be a diluted form of irony, especially when it comes to names. So a hypothetical weathergirl named 'June Blizzard' is considered slightly ironic by many, even though it is often more of a truism than an irony (depending on the weather) under the strict definition. But we don't only consider the strict irony of the vertically challenged 'John Tallman', most people extend the definition. Mr Tallman can be extremely tall and that's considered ironic too.

So the thousand and one people who say that Morissette's lyrics are not ironic can never quite be sure that they are right. Because other people do see irony there. Maybe the biggest irony is that the lyrics really are ironic after all. Irony makes fools of us all. Or at least those who talk about it. Those with an inner irony sensor will sometimes describe it as being like an extra sense. Maybe that is an exaggeration, but it is generally supposed to be better to understand irony than not to.

I'm not saying that a person's sensitivity to irony makes a better person. The greatest irony is that those who see and use irony can be the cruellest people. It is elitist to make any kind of value judgement. Oscar Wilde may say that irony is 'wasted on the stupid', but Wilde was as subject to it as the rest of us. A human being's worth is not measured by his or her understanding of irony.

All kinds of people can be incredibly sensitive to irony and being able to see it does not make someone a better person. Or a worse one. Some people can see irony where others can't and this does not necessarily mean that those who do not see it are somehow lessened. If a conscience is sometimes likened to an internal compass then what should a person's understanding of irony be likened to? I would suggest that it is a sword, because it is used as a weapon in debate. In terms of survival, it really is better to recognise irony.

What I am saying is that being able to see these ironies is a major advantage, even when it seems to be a disadvantage. Irony can be like a secret joke which, if unexplained, can be highly effective in debate, in conversation and in life. There are pragmatic implications to seeing irony. Those who wield this sword want others to see it swinging through the air. They want their enemies to be completely ignorant of the severing blow which has just occurred in a conversation. There is a pride in the wielding of irony. And that, in itself is ironic – as I will attempt to show.

In real life it is slightly different, as we do not see a person holding the sword. The sword may be there, but the one who swings the sword is invisible. 'Don't take this personally,' says irony personified.

And of course, the recognition of ironies can be like vinegar to the wounds which life can inflict. Those of us who feel the sting understand that it seems to be highly personal in nature.

For example, if you claim that you are a genius and the best person at your job the day before your boss fires you, it all feels a little personal. Importantly, I don't want to suggest that these events are true divine irony. If you are following the possible conclusions of irony in life being the product of an ironist then you have probably already figured out where such an idea would lead. Divine irony may be caused by God but I would argue that it is only positive in nature. Okay, that's a bit of a cop out – am I really going to say that all good ironies come from God and all bad ironies come from the devil? Not quite. What we consider to be divine irony is not always divine irony. I will go into this in further depth later. Importantly, there is a difference between irony being caused and being *allowed* by God.

And all this is without even going into the major ironies which litter our lives. Major ironies which we miss. But which others can often see, like the pop-psychology Johari Window segment we can't see through, but others can.

The most obvious question in my premise is this: *If the irony of fate is evidence for a creator – then what does that say about the character of that creator?*

There is a kind of madness to the assertion and irony itself can turn all kinds of words into gobbledegook. So I will try to be as clear as possible and not anthropomorphise or personify irony too much. However, if irony itself were personified I would guess that it would not be an entirely benevolent entity.

I am claiming that the existence of ironies implies an ironist. That irony has a number of sources – human, accidental and yes, supernatural. That there is a person behind the ironies which occur, which we are so unwillingly subject to. And that it really is personal. That it sometimes even has meaning, or at the very least points to the possibility of a meaning. That the ironies which occur in your life, if you see them, are allowed and sometimes even orchestrated. That there is an intelligent ironist. In fact, that there are a number of ironists. I'm not saying that chance and accident don't happen. Sometimes ironic things happen without any other person involved. But not always.

For many people, it is intellectually insulting to say that all ironies are accidental or that they are even an accident of the brain which has evolved to see patterns in events. But as this is the main counter-evidence I will look into this hypothesis later. If there is an ironist then it raises immediate questions about the nature, character and benevolence of that ironist.

If you have noticed any of life's ironies then you will firstly be aware that they are almost always negative. Let me give an example (this is a purposefully trite example because many ironies are painful and I'm not entirely devoid of empathy.

An example…

You are on your way to an important interview for your dream job and your train is delayed. This is known (obviously) as 'Sod's Law' (which is understood and defined as 'everything will always go wrong whatever you do'). Being late throws your carefully prepared plans and you feel upset and stressed. The circumstances feel contrived, but you know that no power can control your movements and the movements of public transport and time it all so well. How could anyone know that today is so important to you? As a result of the delay and the way in which you react, cursing whatever powers have caused this, you are slightly late and when you arrive you are entirely thrown and the interview goes very badly. On top of this, the day before the interview you had asserted to friends: "This interview is in the bag". Hubris. You were unlucky? Should you have simply prepared more? You were confident, not arrogant – and even if you were a little arrogant, what of it? Next time…

If there were a power behind an incident like this then it would need to be a great power. It would need to be a power which can cause trains to be delayed. It would need to be able to hear and understand the language and motive of the confident words spoken the day before. It would need to know what your likely reaction to being late would be. It would need to have planned it all out. It would need to be as close to being omnipotent and omniscient as to be either God or the devil.

Hence the cursing of God if you are an agnostic who has any faith (and blaming God is an act of faith). I would like to bring forward some more evidence that the irony of fate is not a chance accident interpreted by brains which have evolved to see patterns. I would like to claim that irony often really does have a creator. That there is meaning to it all.

Anyone who argues with God knows that we tend to look foolish when we are locked into an argument with God. And there is an irony in this.

Another example…

You can be preparing a meal and thinking about how stingy God, if he really exists, is being towards you, how he rarely seems to let the things happen which you want to happen. He really has been quite vicious to you and cutting, so, 'What do you think of that God, if you are really there?'. And suddenly the knife you are holding slips. You cut your finger because you are locked in a kind of conscious resistance, an ongoing inner argument with the powers that be. And it's your fault. And you know that no-one cares that you were arguing with God in your head (and why be so proud as to think that God was listening to your thoughts anyway?) To try to say that it was God's fault is just going to make you look foolish and you can't prove that. And the worst of it is that God seems to know that. So you look silly and your finger hurts and the war with God continues. A further resentment, filling a lake of resentment towards God within your soul. A continuation of the warfare. A further irony. Especially, because, as everyone knows, we don't have souls in these post-ironic times, we simply have brains and bodies. So God is, as they say, dead and irony is alive but a little jaded.

The evidence for an ironist (and for the soul) is all around us and it has been overlooked. That irony exists is a fact. The question is whether that irony is simply an evolutionary survival mechanism through which the brain creates patterns or if there is a higher meaning to it. If there is any meaning at all to it. That the existence of this irony has any deeper meaning remains debatable. And the reason it is seen as spurious is because of the nature of most ironies.

Chapter 2 - Irony in My Life

Let's take another example because I'm rambling again…

Everything that anyone will ever learn is subjective and experiential. Even objective, logical education is something which is experienced as a person with a life story. That's a nice dogmatic assertion for you to disagree with so that you don't give a fig about me. For now, it's important that you don't like me as an intrusive narrator because we have to analyse part of my life story together.

I have often been tempted to stop being a Christian. Christians say, 'It is a decision you will never regret', but perhaps what they mean is that you will never be able to say you regret it. The main reason I haven't 'moved on' from my 'Christian phase' is because of irony. Because the existence of continuing ironies in my personal life have persuaded me that, in all likelihood, God exists. When I looked at my faith, I realised that the foremost, sustaining reason that I believed in God was because of the ironic (and often unlucky) events which took place every single day.

And so, because stories make the world go 'round, to a story of hubris and nemesis. Of excessive pride and humiliation. In the summer of 1995, if you had been there (and let's hope you weren't), you may have found me in a music store in Stafford, England listening on some 90's music store headphones to a CD by Alanis Morissette called *Jagged Little Pill*. No-one watching would have been able to hear the song *Ironic* begin as I gazed vacantly, glassy eyed, spaced out, into the street. And no-one else would know that this ghostly 23 year old man was an inpatient of the local mental institution who had to be back in hospital by 8pm before the doors were locked to keep the inmates inside and the sane outside.

In literature, any narrative written by someone with a sanity that is under question is usually said to be the story of an unreliable narrator. Hence we have Poe's *The Tell-Tale Heart* and a host of other stories narrated by characters who are not to be trusted. Please remember the distinction between narrator and author here, because I would like to refer back to this subject in later chapters (when I venture into out and out madness (as usual)).

The irony of being diagnosed with a mental health problem was that a little while before the diagnosis, I had taken great pride in my intellect. I had decided that my brain was the one thing I could rely on. I'd been quite confident about that. Arrogant even. As it turned out, my brain, and even my conscience was faulty. My conscience like a compass spinning in all directions at once. And my brain like a useless soggy, sponge in the head.

I largely understood the concept of irony as a child. Reading the comic *Whizzer and Chips* and the *Bumpkin Billionaires*, I understood that it was 'funny, strange' for a cartoon family always to be wanting to get rid of their money. That as soon as they succeeded in getting rid of their fortune in the comic strip they always somehow came into more money than they had before, against their wishes. It was a kind of irony in reverse to real life where instead of wanting to make money, the Bumpkin family wanted to lose theirs (and yet they would never, ever succeed, always winning the lottery or finding some invaluable treasure after they threw their sacks of cash into the sea).

Up until the age of ten I never had a word for such things, but I understood the concept well enough. Children understand a lot more than adults think. And so when, aged 11 my English teacher explained the definition of irony, I immediately thought, 'Well, obviously'. I understood the literal and the literary definition. And I understood the everyday definition of irony in day-to-day life. At least I thought I did. Children can and do understand the concept of irony. Like adults they are subject to the rules or laws of irony. The weather always seems to turn bad as soon as the school holidays begin. And this kind of pattern is played out in many aspects of all our lives, adult or child. On the whole, children understand. But we forget that we once understood and think we learned it. An understanding of irony is within the minds of children from birth. Later I'll talk a little about whether this is an evolutionary survival mechanism.

My understanding of irony rusted as I grew older, like a sword which is left in the rain and never cared for. When I was a teenager I became proud of my intellect. I was in the top sets at school and although I may not have been a genius, I did feel that I could take any issue, any subject and sort it out in my head. I vividly remember one day lying on my bed as young man and thinking, *'My mind is the one thing that I can always rely on'*. I had that ugly condescension towards those who were less intelligent (and why is imagination rarely measured when it comes to intelligence?)

In the Old Testament there is a story about Nebuchadnezzar, the king of Babylon, becoming incredibly proud of his power and influence. Such stories are re-enacted today in smaller ways. It is said that the world gives birth to people who are less great than their forefathers as time goes on.

Nebuchadnezzar exclaims, at the height of his power, *'Look how great Babylon is! I built it as my capital city to display my power and might, my glory and majesty.'*

Daniel 4:28

A few days later the biblical story has it that he goes mad and ends up homeless, eating grass like an animal, losing his kingdom and power. Whether or not you consider the Bible to be fiction or not, it is still a fact that people's lives tend to follow the pattern of the old proverb, 'pride comes before a fall'. It is also considered by some that there is a spiritual law in which the proud are humbled and vice versa.

Before our proverb were the words of Christ who either observed or created the law that the proud would be humbled and the humble would be honoured. Eventually. Most Christians would say that he created it. There is an ironic aspect to this. King Nebuchadnezzar lost his kingdom and his mind. He lived in the wild and this is now known as one of the few depictions of mental illness in the Bible.

Although I was very proud of my intellect I was clearly not wise, as I took a medley of drugs at university and these drugs had a knock-on effect which I believe resulted in later metal health problems. So, during the summer of '95, pumped full of prescribed antipsychotic drugs, I came to realise that my mind was something which I could not always rely on at all. And I lifted my eyes to heaven and I was not healed. My mind, my logic and my conscience appeared to be faulty.

I had already been baptised in a church as I had been a Christian for over two years at that point. After the baptism, before the sectioning, I was given a scripture which read, 'Lean not on your own understanding'. And I took it as a kind of message from God.

So, to be so proud of my intellect and then to realise that I could not always trust my mind was deeply humbling. And ironic. And seeing all that didn't heal me either. It just acted as vinegar to a wound.

There is a power to irony because the understanding of it can be elitist. This may not ultimately sort the chaff from the wheat (and why would anyone want to?) but the fact is that a lot of good people will not see ironies where others can see them. This turns it into a secret cipher for the intelligent. This is what made Socrates so powerful in debate. He would ask a seemingly innocent question and defeat his opponents with a feigned naivety. He pretended to be humble and simple in order to win debates. Like Columbo does in his, "Just one last thing..." sentence as he begins to leave a murderer's house. And it is often still the knock-out blow in an internet debate. Use irony and your opponent will not only look simple, but you will have brought your audience along with you (providing you are not a total ar*e). You will win the argument. At least among the ironically enlightened.

Or if no-one else gets the irony, you will have the personal satisfaction of knowing that you won. And no-one will think you have won. And that will be ironic too.

I have never won an Internet debate in my life. I'm of the old-school opinion that you can't win an argument. Of course, I could just be lying to win an argument in saying that, because this book is one long, confusing claim. Remember that I must be an unreliable narrator as I have a certificate in madness (which even the NHS recognises). Also, there is an irony in failing to win in debate and then attempting to put forward this kind of theory. But some arguments cannot be won or lost, even if they are important. For a person to debate that God exists in a persuasive way, they must win the person and not necessarily the argument. And I'm worried I have simply alienated you through clumsy and dogmatic assertions.

Maybe Christ proved that not being able to win an argument is a nonsense idea because he never backed away from robust debate and clearly saw some purpose in debating moot points. But I'm not Christ (that much should be very obvious), I'm a sinner and I don't have to have the same opinions as Christ has. Alienate your audience and no-one wins. All you end up proving is that you are a total shmuck. They say that there is a reason that you can't prove God. And that is because the outrageous irony is that God doesn't want to be proved yet. Well, there's further irony for you.

'That's very convenient', you may be thinking. But you can't prove or disprove God. I challenge you to even try to do one or the other before the end of the world. God doesn't want to be proved, he wants to be believed in. 'Very, very convenient.' And that is why all manner of spiritual forces will either aid or prevent any attempt to prove God. Including this one. But what can be done is to bring new evidence forward. And that is why I am attempting (perhaps badly) to present irony as a serious example of the existence of a higher power.

Anyone who recognises irony in their life will know that any God who orchestrates such ironies would have to be, as Stephen Fry put it so eloquently, a monstrous 'capricious, mean-minded, stupid God', an 'utter maniac'. Irony is much greater evidence for the devil than for God. If it is evidence at all, it is evidence for an intelligent, personal, cruel power.

Irony is of such a nature that it needs to blind some to its working and open the eyes of others. At least literary irony must do this. We must know that the pride of Dr Frankenstein will result in his downfall even when he doesn't. That the creature he proudly creates and which he believes will astonish the world and bring him fame will become his nemesis. And literary irony is similar to the irony of fate when it takes place within the life stories of real characters. The irony of fate is that power which seems to orchestrate events to the most ironic outcome.

And so, to another subjective example to show how unsuited I am to this task. But a book without stories is hard to read…

When I took up my journalism training I was often sent to find stories to write up for the student magazine.

I was staying in dingy pub accommodation, sharing a room with a course mate. Downstairs in the pub were a huge collection of water jugs hanging from hooks, in every nook and cranny available. So it seemed right to talk with the landlord about his water jug collection and write it up as a human interest story for the student newspaper.

As I was writing the story, the course tutor came over to see what I was working on.

"Don't you think that it's ironic that a pub landlord should collect water jugs?" he asked.

I hadn't seen the irony until it was mentioned. What it proved to me was that sometimes, no matter how attuned to irony you feel you are, you are going to miss ironies, especially when you are close to them. Certainly, you shouldn't be proud of your ironic sensitivities. It is tempting fate. But when you feel there are no ironies then that is probably when there are many. This is the nature of irony. It is a hidden pattern in our lives.

In effect, we all, at times, play the part of Alazons, the subject of ironies, the subject of the humiliation of the Eiron. At other times we may be the Eiron. But sometimes we are the braggart opponents, perpetually becoming proud and getting humbled for it. Sometimes we humble others. That is the pattern. How then, to use this pattern pragmatically?

In my 20s I did a lot of work experience on local papers. Before the digital revolution it was seen as the best way to get your name in front of editors. Occasionally it involved more than making tea and coffee for the staff writers or writing up press releases. Sometimes you would shadow reporters on their rounds or find and write your own stories. I desperately wanted to please the editor at The

Stoke *Sentinel* as I had heard that impressing him could lead to a job on the paper. I was born in Stoke and liked the idea of covering my home patch. It was, perhaps, a dream job.

The news editor was an efficient character with a kind of raw energy which came from too much stress and adrenaline, walking around the newsroom with shouts of, "Come on!"

"Where's the work experience guy? Alright, instead of making tea and coffee for us, I'm going to send you to get an important story. This is your big chance, I want you to drive one of our cars to see a Mr Grimly who is at loggerheads with the council over health support. Here's his name and address."

So I took one of the newspaper's cars and drove to the address using an A-Z of the area (it was before the age of Sat Navs). I parked up outside the care home where Mr Grimly had a flat. I entered the care home, and perhaps unprofessionally attempted to find Mr Grimly's room without checking into any kind of informal reception. The care home was a labyrinth with corridors leading in all directions and finding the right door was hard. But I had phoned ahead and knew that Mr Grimly would be expecting me. His raspy old voice had given the impression of a man who didn't care what people thought anymore. He had sounded like an old crow. After a long time I found his door. I rang the door buzzer and waited. And waited. I rang again. After about ten minutes of waiting I realised that he either wasn't going to answer or had gone out. It was before the time of mobiles so I didn't easily have a way of calling him again. As I stood there waiting I looked up at the sign which Mr Grimly had placed to decorate the wall next to his door. It was titled 'Sod's Law' and was a jokey kind of poem about how if anything can go wrong it will. The kind you can pick up at a garden centre if you are tired of life.

On the way out of the care home I got lost and found myself around the back of the huge building. But there was a back door and I could see that it led out along a fenced pathway to a gate and there was a road beyond that. So I went through the door and let it swing shut behind me. When I reached the iron gate I saw that I was locked in. And when I walked back to the door of the home it wouldn't open. I was trapped on a narrow pathway with a high metal fence. No escape for residents this way. So I stood there and as it began to rain I wished I had bought a coat. And mobile phones hadn't been invented. And this was my big break at my dream job. It took me a long time to get anyone's attention to let me back into the home and by the time I got back to the newsroom most people had left. And I had to explain to the news editor that I had not got a story and had been trapped outside. The news editor shrugged and gave me a look as if to say, 'You're not really cut out for this are you?'

Sod's Law is interesting. It tends to be believed largely by older people, by those who have a bit more experience of life. They say: 'When people age they can turn into a fine wine. But most turn to vinegar'. And there is a reason for this.

Life has a habit of kicking dreams from our grasp and so Sod's Law gains its believers. The Americans have a relatively positive version of the phenomenon and they call it 'Murphy's Law' - a law which isn't quite so fatalistic, a law which can be defeated with adequate preparation. It states that 'if anything can go wrong, it will', but there is a concession that only the things which can go wrong will go wrong, so an individual can prepare and prevent many bad things from happening through foresight. The British version is called Sod's Law – and this is a law of nature, perhaps influenced by our often depressing weather, which cannot be defeated no matter how hard you try. Attempting to stop Sod's Law from occurring simply makes it more likely to happen - it is a much more fatalistic version of Murphy's Law and a lot more pessimistic.

Sod's Law and Murphy's Law are almost always ironic in nature. They influence all aspects of life. Not believing in them makes no difference, they happen anyway. Even to the Pollyannas. They are not always (but can be) self-fulfilling prophecies. They have no logic. It's when you want fish and chips and the guy in front of you orders the last fish. It's found in the phone call when you're in the bath. It isn't very ironic, but it is a little ironic. Bad luck can be ironic.

This has been a pattern within my life. Pride coming before a fall. But humility never seeming to come before any kind of honour. I currently believe in Murphy's Law, but there is still time to fall into out and out fatalism. I choose Murphy's Law over Sod's Law as it implies some kind of hope. And most of us are prisoners of hope (or at least of the hope in a future hope).

Murphy's Law has even been said to be one of the laws of thermodynamics - according to some scientists. Other scientists, such as Richard Dawkins strongly disagree that this 'law' even exists. Dawkins states that Sod's Law and Murphy's Law are simply a form of confirmation bias – that, if, (to quote Alanis once again) you have 'rain on your wedding day', it is because you notice it more rather than because it is important to you. It rains all the time, but this time it may or may not have been important for you that there was no rain for wedding photographs. And certainly no storm. And if it seems that the sun shines on everyone else's wedding day, that too is confirmation bias, without meaning and devoid of rhyme or reason. Scientists noticing that plans and experiments failing have an almost supernatural habit of happening has little scientific basis beyond the second law of thermodynamics, the law of entropy – the tendency of things to move to a more disorganised state. And if other scientists like Dawkins debunk such ideas, then that can't be Sod's Law can it, for those scientists that have noticed it? Because it is suggesting that this law is active in all spheres of life, including the world of science. Like gravity.

Or if, for example, it seems that when children break up for their summer holidays that the skies always turn grey and the sun hides his face (having been smiling on the children through the windows of their shady classrooms during term-time) then that is simply confirmation or selection bias. It is what we notice and it simply seems to be a law of thermodynamics, a law of nature. If there really were a Murphy's Law then it would simply be a way that things are – that this is a law of nature without any intelligent force behind it. You could say that God causes it (as it is in keeping with the malevolent petty image of God who seems to be out to get us) or you could, during kinder moments simply think that it is something which God allows but doesn't cause.

The whole subject is a minefield, full of all kinds of ways to look silly or else to be crass and insensitive. To suggest that God controls the weather or allows the weather when so many people all around the world are subject to weather conditions which really are a matter of life and death. When the sun causes skin cancer ('God damn the sun'). How can anyone state that God doesn't at least allow these things even if he doesn't cause them? Where is the conscience of God when a house is flooded? What is more godly – the act of nature or those who help in the circumstances?

But isn't it simply sycophancy to suggest that God only does good and that he has no responsibility for what we call 'Acts of God'? How can an individual psychologically survive believing that God is causing storms to take lives or volcanoes to erupt or earthquakes to destroy? And is it even possible to make an adequate defence of God in those circumstances? Doing so will only keep God clean and pristine, it will only keep his reputation unsullied – and what is the point of that? Does God really need defending anyway? Can't he defend himself? Does he need a million and one people to defend his honour as if he is some fair maiden who has been horribly misrepresented by some enemy? And if God doesn't need defending for the things that he allows, why are there a million and one willing hands and voices who would defend him? And if a person is to defend God's honour for the things he allows then are they acting out of fear or out of love? Or do they simply hope that in the defending of God they will receive preferential treatment on this earth? Is the whole subject a minefield? And in the asking these questions, have I confused both you and myself? That's Murphy's Law for you.

I am writing the end of this chapter sitting on a bench at a major university in the UK. My wife works here as a careers consultant. Yesterday she gave an interview to the local BBC radio station about how this university won the best student employability award from The Times. In the background the university clock let's out a low, authoritative bong as if to say, '*Work, study, compete*'.

I'm here for a training session for a role I have as a notetaker for disabled students. It's a part time role which is satisfying enough. But there is no job security. I currently don't even know if I have any hours to work next week. It is a transitory job and even though it is officially temp work, at seven years it is the longest job I've ever had. My wife is both proficient and successful at her job and has helped many students to find work. And yet her husband struggles to find work. Once again I missed this irony for a while until one of my wife's students pointed it out to me. I suppose I'm her greatest challenge (in more ways than one). It proves that we have a blind spot when it comes to irony in our own lives.

That both our needs and desires are subject to Murphy's Law.

What I am trying to show is that the important thing to understand about irony is that the major ironies will almost always revolve around health, career choice, major life events, significant others and names (although sometimes locations and timings can be involved).

My full name is Nicholas Christian White. I am Christian and White, although I still don't wear knickers (whatever my schoolmates may have said). The name Nicholas comes from the Greek word 'Nike' – meaning victory and 'las' meaning people.

One of my convictions is that the people are the ones who need to be heard and considered above leaders and politicians. So it could be considered a truism, depending on how far I speak up for people. Or perhaps, if I act as devil's advocate – just 'old Nick'. Not so much a truism towards my namesake, I can assure you.

That's not ironic,' intones the university clock bell as if to comment on the thought.

Chapter 3 - Irony in Names

"Remember that a person's name is to that person the sweetest and most important sound in any language."

Dale Carnegie

Any ironist loves names. Authors play with the names of characters all the time, often using them as truisms or as ironic contradictions to their character. So many pieces of classical literature from Bunyan through to Dickens will have characters within them who mirror their names or who somehow fulfil (or spectacularly fail to fulfil their name's meaning).

There is also a case of art mirroring real life. Although many people named 'Joy' will be as happy as can be expected, there are also many Joys who are depressed and who feel that their name is a mockery of its meaning. If your name is Joy I apologise if this example is ironic in itself.

It's like the surname of the fastest man on the planet being 'Bolt'. But how are such things evidence for anything apart from our ability to find patterns within language? How is the seeming evolutionary ability to see irony within names an indication of any deeper meaning?

The ability to use language for alliteration, poetry, simile, metaphor and irony are intrinsic to the human condition. The New Testament event goes so far as to call Christ 'The Word made flesh'. This linking together of language and life is taken for granted. If God does not speak in any understandable language then why do scriptures of religions contain irony within them? I would theorise that it is because God understands irony, because we were created to understand irony for a purpose.

The Bible is fond of using name meanings to act as both truisms and ironic contradictions.

For example, King Herod's name means 'Hero' and 'Song'. If there was any character who was less of a hero and whose life was anything but a song then it was of King Herod, the man who was responsible for the massacre of babies. The name 'Judas' stems from 'Judah' meaning 'Praises'. Few characters have been praised less than Judas Iscariot (who himself, seemed to offer a strange kind of praise in his life). Even the name 'Mary' can mean 'Rebelliousness' and the mother of Christ is held as the perfect example of obedience (at least to God).

Many of the other names in the Bible are truisms – Abraham means 'Father of many'. Esau means 'hairy'. Adam means 'man'. Israel means 'God contended (or he who contends with God)'. Saul means 'Asked for'.

The Bible is not supposed to be read as a work of fiction (it is supposed to be a mixture of history, parable, allegory, prophecy and poetry). But just as the classics will have an ironist in their authors, real life implies an Author. It implies that we, as characters, are not entirely the masters of our fates and captains of our souls (as much as we may hate this idea). Literature has ironists in its authors, narrators and sometimes in its characters. Real life has an Ironist in an Author. Names can be given by chance, they can be picked out of baby-name lists (as most people's names are). The implication is that accident and chance are the only ironists here. That our names (which can also be changed, either through marriage or through deed poll) are not entirely accidental.

Not everyone is entirely reconciled with their present name. Consider your own name. Is it entirely without irony?

Chapter 4 – Isn't it Ironic?

Back to examples…

I'll have to use my own life as this is the main source as it is less likely to have me blunder into rubbing vinegar into wounds. Human beings are by nature subjective and irony in your own life, when you see it, is the most compelling evidence of an ironist. I am proposing that when there is an ironist there is more than one ironist. Powers which metaphorically write irony into people's lives are not necessarily God. 'It ain't necessarily so' as the song goes.

So here's another relatively tame example which I hope you can associate with. Once again it may fall into a kind of Murphy's Law category, the kind of category which includes a phone call as soon as you get into the bath. Remember that the major ironies involve your name, occupation, major life events and death. They can also revolve around timings and locations. And if irony is to be understood, in literature and in life, it needs an audience. And a story.

Here's a little irony relating to coincidence or synchronicity. My wife and I had a pet guinea pig named 'Mr Darcy' (after the Pride and Prejudice character). He died suddenly and we buried him in the garden in a mobile phone box. There was a short service and a few words to mark his passing across the rainbow bridge. It was all very sad. The same day I received an email about a new book with the name 'Mr Darcy' in the title. It seemed at the time like a negative experience, a kind of mockery rather than a comfort.

A further example – At the time of writing our cat, Molly, has just died at the age of 18. Suddenly there are cats everywhere I look. We had her cremated and as we waited to pick up the ashes there was a local news item about pets ashes not being genuine and of negligence in that area. Then there were the news reports of cat rescue centres wanting more people to take in new cats. This is perhaps the way that life works, although these kind of things can act as intimate, unwelcome blows. Then there were the letters from the pet store addressed to 'Molly' offering vouchers for cat food. The kind of blows that most people are used to when suffering any kind of grief.

This kind of irony or synchronicity is said to relate to something called the Baader-Meinhof phenomenon. Supposedly, part of the brain is activated to look for a particular thing and then confirmation bias kicks in, causing it to appear as if this thing is everywhere you look. You will probably hear of Baader-Meinhof wherever you look now (especially if you visit the Facebook page dedicated to this phenomenon). It is said to be a very natural psychological phenomenon which is proved by millions of people. But why is it there? What is the evolutionary purpose of it?

It is very similar to the ancient teaching of Christ, 'Seek and ye shall find'. And whether this seeking is conscious or unconscious, we often tend to find what we are looking for. It is almost as though the Baader-Meinhof phenomenon was not as original a theory as was supposed. Of course, the irony is that so many of us complain that people look for the bad in us and then we go on to look for the bad in others, all the time complaining, 'You noticed that I did this wrong, but what about all these things I did right?' And we make the same (seemingly valid) complaint of God – that he only looks for the things we do wrong, not the things we do right.

I noticed the Baader-Meinhof phenomenon when I was a little boy and was watching a programme called 'Crown Court' at home. It had a judge in it but I didn't know what a 'judge' was. And suddenly, sure as a gavel hitting me on the head, 'judges' were everywhere I looked. I wasn't consciously looking for them, at least at first. But suddenly all around me were people talking about judges, judges in the news, judges wherever I looked and whatever I read. It was as if a highlighter had been placed on the subject.

This phenomenon is also linked with synchronicity and serendipity and although left brained thinkers would prefer to call it an evolutionary peculiarity, the spiritual tend to see synchronicity in terms of signs from a higher power.

Thinking people everywhere will often wonder if there is more to it than the perception of patterns. Often we will put it down to life itself, or cause and effect, but when the irony is personal or intimate, it does seem to have a mind of its own. And if it is just a function of the human brain, who decided that it should be there? And why would it be there? Recognising irony doesn't always help us to survive, sometimes it does the opposite. Sometimes it tempts us to give up.

The problem with the theory that there is no great ironist is the problem of experience. In life and in literature there is an audience who understand irony when it is played out in the lives of the characters around them (or there may only be an audience of one). Most of us who experience irony, or, at least, those of us who sometimes recognise it (bearing in mind that it is the nature of irony to be missed), will understand that when an irony 'happens to us', it is usually negative. So, at the very least, the Baader-Meinhof phenomenon seems to deliberately 'delude' people into believing that the phenomenon is some kind of message or sign. It is like the way the sinister conscience character deals with Joan when she is in a prison in the film *The Messenger: The Story of Joan of Arc*. She considers a sword she has seen, which she has always believed to be a sign from God. 'That was a sign', says Joan. 'No', says her conscience darkly, 'that was a sword'.

So does anyone orchestrate the ironies?

I believe that as in literature, ironies in life can either be accidents, or orchestrated by one Author, one antagonist, or occasionally some of the characters. In literature of course, there are few accidents.

People make mistakes. There are huge ironies in people's lives which are often negative and which cause intense personal suffering. It follows, or at least seems, that any personal force behind these things is powerful and oppressive.

What if some ironies really were orchestrated by a benevolent God? A good and merciful God?

"But if that is true - then the higher power is a shmuck and an ar*e!" you could understandably say. And the most important thing in those circumstances would be to mount a human campaign against such a power, if it is possible. To remove all love, all praise and all communication towards such a power. An ironist who thinks it is ironic for a country to suffer a disaster just when it is finding its feet or an ironist who causes an individual to suffer an illness just when they think everything is going well. To win the lottery and 'die the next day' as Alanis said.

But, to repeat myself, the problem is that we are assuming that the ironies have been *caused* by this power rather than *allowed* by this power. In terms of literature, there is an author and usually an antagonist and the two are distinct if the author is competent (and has any tenuous link on sanity).

So with fiction, as with life. These kind of ironies are allowed but they are negative, at least most of us experience them negatively. Yet, the ironies still seem to point to a personality who understands our personal lives and how events will influence us.

The character of the antagonist may take over a narrative within a story for a while. At this point this voice is not necessarily that of the author. What I'm trying to say is that we mistake some ironies as being the acts of God. God has only allowed them. He hasn't caused or willed them. For example, in a story, an author can write in the first person as the antagonist, allowing the antagonist to control events - this is not necessarily the voice of the author. That is the voice of the narrator who the author has created.

Now try to apply this to your life. Such an outside narrative voice could, in theory, be allowed, or be given the power to make you suffer cruel ironies. You would blame the author. This narrator would be very happy about this. The author is only to be blamed in that he or she has *allowed* the antagonist to orchestrate the irony of fate.

So this is my core argument. Good ironies come from God. Bad ironies don't. Good ironies, serendipity, happy, lucky meetings, and the right idea at the right time – these are willed by God. 'Very, very, convenient' I hear you think again. But few people would say that life is so unendurable as not to contain any good ironies.

I'm defending God and to an extent he doesn't need defending. I have only come to this conclusion because it is the only coping mechanism that does not tear my fragile psyche in two. I cannot compute a God who causes negative ironies. I cannot compute a God who causes suffering.

This, I'm sure, is all very predictable coming from a believer. So I need to provide some evidence that the good things that happen come from God. I will attempt to do that. There is, strangely, some evidence for it.

The existence of irony is evidence for the existence of ironists. The character of the ironists is in question. If the resulting ironies are cruel then we would automatically assume that the character of the ironist is that of being a horrific bully and an oppressor. However, there is a distinction. The Author doesn't escape responsibility for allowing the negative events to take place. But the Author hasn't **caused** the negative events. The Author has simply *allowed* them.

At this point it looks as if I'm going to engage in the usual spiel of suggesting that the Author (God) has no responsibility. But that is insulting to most thinking human beings and we naturally rebel against that idea. All I'm suggesting is that the Author is not malevolent. If the Author has a fault it is at least the appearance of negligence, not cruelty.

Here's the theory again…

The existence of a cruel, oppressive antagonist automatically suggests the existence of an author. It suggests this because this is what we hold to be true since childhood - you can't just have evil - there has to be good too. Some people say that good needs evil. The ironist tends to be oppressive and causes great pain. These are the hallmarks of evil – of a devil. Therefore the existence of an ironist as a personality infers the existence of an evil power who is sometimes allowed to do this. The existence of a personal evil automatically suggests the existence of God. The existence of God is further to be hinted at in love and in good ironies. This is the pattern on the wing of the butterfly. This is the face in the tree or the shape in the cloud.

The trouble with this theory is that some ironies clearly could not be orchestrated by the devil. It is blaming the devil for every single cruel irony – a throwing away of personal responsibility. The devil can't make it rain on weddings. So how, theologically, can anyone get around this without stating the blindingly obvious? God orchestrates irony too. For evidence of this I will look at the life of someone who both was subject to and used irony against others. The relevance of this particular figure will give further insights into who is to blame. The blame game is not entirely fruitless. Sometimes it is necessary in order to solve a problem.

As you can see, this book has driven me quite loopy and superstitious. This has been a dry and confusing chapter. So let's move on to out and out madness…

Chapter 5 - A Demon Named Irony

Prove irony and you have good evidence for a devil or some other malevolent entity. Please indulge me in my superstition here. I'm among the last of my kind in believing (as people used to do years ago) that each person has a personal angel and a personal demon. William Golding's *Lord of the Flies* is an excellent classic story which contains irony and has a theme of evil being within us rather than outside us. Golding told the story of children trying to survive on an island, fearful of an evil 'beast'. But there was no beast. The evil was only within human nature. But if there really were a devil that is exactly the conclusion he would want you to draw.

Because ironic events are almost always negative, if there is a power acting as an ironist it has to be malevolent. Surely? But prove the devil and you don't necessarily prove God. Although it's a start. Only someone on a bad LSD trip or in a drug-induced psychosis would believe that the devil ruled the world. The idea that we could be living in a kind of gnostic nightmare in which there is no loving God is not taken seriously because of the existence of love and hope. Even dualism would have it that there are equally powerful forces for good and evil. It is too bleak to believe that the devil rules the world. Few people believe that the 'truth' could be that the devil is playing with every one of us and when we die there is only a devil and no God. And the disturbing 'truth', in this case, would be that we have a series of dark epiphanies as we come to realise that all the suffering and the evil which we experience is the product of a cruel mastermind. Tolstoy may have feared that his life was a celestial joke from some powerful enemy, but he moved on from that fear. I'm not suggesting it is the truth, although I am suggesting that the urban myth of an immensely powerful devil is a piece of the truth. But that is not the whole truth.

Proving, or at least finding evidence for the devil can be a step towards evidence for God. No-one said you couldn't prove the devil, they just say you can't prove God. A narrator or an antagonist in a book of fiction may hold great power, but the antagonist is not (or perhaps should not be) the author. God allows irony and he allows the devil to exist. The Christian metanarrative has it that God created the devil, we would assume, knowing what he would do in the future. So, it could be said that God allowing the devil to orchestrate cruel ironies makes God negligent. God orchestrating cruel ironies makes God malevolent. It's a nasty minefield once again. And the 'good news' is that according to this story, there are a whole host of demons too.

I would like to claim that the devil does orchestrate some ironies and that God is not cruel. But I won't defend him from the accusation of appearing to be negligent. God can defend himself from that through action. Crucially, my claim is that God does not cause the negative ironies. His 'crime' is simply in allowing them. (But we project the image of our parents and ourselves onto God the father.)

So, to get to the point, I would like to attempt to show how some ironies are so great, and so cruel, that they could only be orchestrated by a malevolent, pernicious and intelligent force. Once again, this doesn't even prove the devil, although it is evidence for an evil entity. Irony is also evidence for demons who understand the concept. It is not so much evidence for a Loki, a trickster god or a kind of chaotic force, although it could be. But it is evidence for evil, personal yet inhuman forces. It is evidence for an intelligent evil. Not necessarily an omnipotent evil, but an evil with many ears and many eyes. Almost as if that evil had a host of demons to delegate to.

We need concrete examples as I am aware that I am straying once again into superstition. Please forgive me for that, but it is a complicated (and dangerous) subject.

Life's ironies take place every day. These include the smaller Murphy's Law ironies, for example of someone else suddenly buying something you had just saved enough money to buy. Or a doctor's appointment clashing with something you really wanted to do (remember that in writing this I am aware that many of these examples can be challenged and obviously you don't have to agree). Furthermore I have no wish to be crass or thoughtless if you are suffering in some ironic way as you read. If you are suffering please be very gentle with yourself. It almost certainly isn't your fault that you are suffering. You haven't brought these ironies on yourself. They just happen. If you aren't suffering then I'll be honest with you – both you and I are going to be suffering again very soon ('Mainly from reading this superstitious, dogmatic nonsense,' I hear you think).

But think about your own experiences. Think about your instincts. Think about your hunches and the way that life treats you. Think about the most important parts of your life story, both the good and the bad. Think about the timings, the people involved and the way in which these scenes unfolded. If you consider these major life events to be simple accidents or only the result of free will or cause and consequence then that's okay. But consider that there may be other forces at work. As Queen Elizabeth said, "There are powers at work in this country about which we have no knowledge." Was she really only talking about the British secret services?

When your flesh crawls for no reason. When you sense evil. When you see the results of evil. When things happen for which there is no rational answer.

How then can I say that there is a devil? Simply look at the cruellest ironies in people's lives. Look at the way people live and die. If there were a creator behind such things in what way could such a creator be called good as we understand this word? Therefore I'm claiming that the orchestrator of the cruellest ironies is sometimes the devil (and/or demons). Clearly most of us are not going to get the attention of Lucifer – what most of us have to put up with is a delegated evil from demons who incite us to make bad decisions. God is the creator of the law of irony, the weapon which is wielded. He created the sword and the one who holds the sword. He does not swing the sword if it is an irony which causes suffering. He does not pour the vinegar into the wound. But for unknown reasons he does allow it. He allows too much.

Ironies are everywhere and the evidence for ironists is all around.

In my time on this earth I have discovered this: It is the agenda or plan of the devil for every human being. His policy is that you either harm other people or you harm yourself. If you take nothing else from this book, please take this. Beyond this he will simply try to make you suffer. If he can do this and be ironic at the same time then he will do that. And there is a reason for this. It doesn't matter if you are a Christian or not. Christians may get more Satanic attack than non-Christians – but everyone suffers because of this external evil. Demons are not flesh and blood. They are not people. They are spiritual beings who can be really nasty.

How do you fight back against something like that? How do you fight back against a cruel ironist? Well, you can start by taking a look at the reasons he uses irony. And that's not just because the devil is a nasty piece of work (although he is that). It is because he is subject to irony too.

As if we do not have enough to deal with without the existence of these entities which want to take us back to the dark ages (incidentally, that's not projection). So let's get God's bad idea of the devil and demons out of the way…

Chapter 6 - Irony in the Devil's Life

Irony, seemingly, is so negative an experience to many of us that it couldn't be orchestrated by God. I understand that this sounds like mental gymnastics, that I'm seeming to be jumping through hoops not to blame God for bad things. If God has a conscience (and we would assume that he does because most of us do), then he has to take responsibility in the same way that we are called to take responsibility.

See how God is more interesting than the devil? Who would most of us prefer to meet?

Some irony can only be orchestrated by a pernicious and malevolent power. Cruel, tragic things like an aspiring author committing suicide the day before an acceptance from a publisher or agent. These ironies are like a kind of Excalibur, a sword wielded by evil personified. A sword lined with poison. Notice that I am using the weaponry metaphor for irony throughout this book and that is deliberate. Irony is not a gentle healing balm. It can sting. It is not always wielded by the 'good'.

So please imagine that the devil exists for a chapter. It's medieval. It's superstitious. It's dogmatic. It's simplistic. And, in the light of the events in this world in which we live, it's the only thing that makes sense. After that we can return to less disturbing topics.

It makes a kind of sense that the devil could orchestrate irony given that, according to both urban myth, popular culture and scripture he is supposed to possess great power. The hubris of Lucifer (commonly understood to be Satan before his fall) becoming so proud as to demand worship and then to be humiliated into being thrown out of heaven is not simply a tale from Milton's *Paradise Lost*. It is a narrative shared by Judaism, Christianity and Islam.

But I'm assuming too much. I'm assuming that you believe in a malevolent power who desires less than the best for you. So, as any atheist would tell me, the burden of proof is on me. I have to persuade you that sometimes, irony comes from the devil. And the best way to do that is to show that the devil (or demons (after all, few of us get personal attention from this most violent, hypocritical tyrant)) uses irony to make things worse for us. Demons may have no legitimate rights (and they don't), but they do have a power. I will try to explain why that might be.

One of the few sources which limit the extent of the devil's power are folk stories in which he is thwarted by wily old 'sinners'. In the folk stories the devil ends up building bridges and getting fooled into promising to take the soul of the first to cross the bridge (usually getting fooled into taking the soul of a dog in exchange for the bridge). But in modern urban myth and the horror genre he is almost supremely powerful. In scripture he can only be defeated by the blood of Christ or by the kind of superhuman endurance and resistance shown by Job. Believers tend to view the devil as a kind of celestial bully who will not take no for an answer, who will kick you when you are down and who delights in your suffering. So when we don't get the dream job or some other irony occurs, it is all kinds of demons which are laughing. It would not be a hard thing for a demon to make you proud, or to make you late, or to cause you to be in the wrong place at the wrong time.

But aside from the disturbing possibility of there being far too many demons, why would the devil orchestrate irony? How does irony prove the devil? It partly proves it from the nature of many ironies. They are often beyond the realms of chance. It is harder to believe that they have happened by accident because they appear to be so well orchestrated.

Firstly we need to look into irony in the life of the devil. And irony used as a projection of personal pain or vengeance. Irony as hypocrisy or, as the proverb goes, 'The pot calling the kettle black.'

According to the threadbare understanding which humans have of the devil's life story, he was created in the beginning as an angel. A major irony in the life of Lucifer in *Paradise Lost* and a few verses of the Bible was that he displayed great hubris, meaning, of course, that he became excessively proud. The ancient Greeks understood that each act of hubris brings its own kind of nemesis. For the devil, his nemesis was God, and God in Christ.

In the Christian community Lucifer is said to have been created as a kind of 'worship leader', as a beautiful and powerful angel with a role in the presence of God. The role, or at least the name of the role, being that of 'bright morning star' – and whatever that involved. According to legend, the devil became proud. Sources differ only slightly in the narrative on this. Muslims, who also see the devil as their enemy, believe that the devil was proud in that he refused to bow down to man, when man was created by God. Other ancient sources see it more as a kind of proud rebellion and an attempt to usurp God's throne. Lucifer becomes proud, as the bright morning star, and it is this pride which is the sin which leads to his downfall. One way or the other Lucifer is thrown out of heaven (falling 'like lightning') and he takes a third of the angels with him. These fallen angels become demons and Lucifer loses his job and his former state. And the demons lose their jobs and angelic states too.

In the book of Revelation, Christ says that he has taken over this heavenly role as the bright morning star. 'I am the bright morning star,' he says at the end of the Bible. Without going into the disturbing, gnostic and inaccurate ideas that God is the devil and vice versa, it would seem that the devil lost his job and his boss replaced him with his son (or with himself if you believe that Christ is God). And it is a similar story for all demons in the whole mythology – that the state or role of demons today is a huge demotion from their original positions.

This is a bitter irony for the devil – and for the demons. Not only did Lucifer lose his job in heaven, but the person who sacked him gave his job to his son. What nepotism it must seem. And not being able to incarnate on earth as his old boss managed to do. Not yet anyway. The pot calling the kettle black when it comes to not turning up. According to the mythology, there really is an irony in the devil specialising in preventing the legitimate desire of parents to have children of their own. Conception is an issue which the devil is struggling with too – the consensus being that he has been unable to have a child of his own. And even if he may manage to have a child at the end of the world, it is not an understatement to suggest that this prophesied child will not entirely have succeeded in being a loving, whole human being. He will fail at this very basic level.

Of course, I'm being disingenuous here. Anyone who has struggled to conceive or who has lost a job only to be replaced by someone they dislike has not necessarily invoked the wrath of Satan or his demons. Often it is just a result of the way things are in this world. Or of the Fall, if you believe any of the Genesis creation story (even as an allegory).

Unemployment usually seems to have a more natural cause. We have responsibilities and we play our parts in that. If God exists then these things are allowed by him and we are back to the circular argument about suffering. But if the devil exists, then these things can be said to be caused by him – or at least delegated to his demons. And there is an irony in that. In that the devil and demons inflict the same suffering on humanity which they have experienced.

So, according to the story of creation, which could well be an allegory, the devil somehow persuaded humanity to fall in a similar way as he did. They too, desired to be gods and they too displayed hubris. Misery loves company. And so it has been since the story of the Fall, the devil continually projecting his own bitterness on this event in making sure that as many people as possible lose their jobs or their positions of security. Unemployment is one of the devil's favourite things (along with violence and prejudice). And if a job role can be taken by an enemy, then how much sweeter the revenge for the ironist.

To continue with the idea that the devil has irony in his life story, in popular Christian tradition the devil possesses a snake in the Garden of Eden and persuades Adam and Eve to sin. This is unlikely to be literal and let's not demonise snakes (as the Bible says, 'Our battle is not against flesh and blood'). It was some kind of temptation which we as the children of Adam and Eve naturally will repeat as a kind of pattern. We can blame the parents as much as we like but most of us who have lived a little will already have made similar mistakes.

So as a result, the snake is punished and cursed. Satan has further powers removed and a prophecy is given that one of Eve's descendants will defeat him. What a bitter irony for the devil that it would be a mortal man, a being who Lucifer refused to bow to, who delivers the crushing blow (at Calvary).

But the heel can still be struck. Lucifer, it seems, is created with an understanding of irony, along with many of the more intelligent fallen angels. That an angel who was so beautiful, so powerful and so honoured should be so humbled is a continuing bitter irony for the devil. Lucifer the light-bearer no more, even his name is an irony, seeming to mock him. Although there may be light of a kind it is a dim distortion of real truth. No longer a light for the world, even that role has been taken away from him and he is now called the Prince of Darkness. Others have taken his job once again. And so his new name becomes a truism, Satan – accuser, adversary – and his old name becomes a mockery of what he once was. He does what his new name says and accuses and acts as an enemy to both God and man. In modern understanding these truisms can also be ironic. As I mentioned earlier, even though they are not the reverse of their meaning they are still considered to be ironic by many. Especially when there has been a name change. I will look into this further with other names, because, as I've noted, irony is particularly active when it comes to names, births, deaths, health conditions and occupations. I will also try to be a bit more grounded once I've got the devil out of the way.

So the end of the devil, according to scriptural prophecy, is that he will be destroyed by a simple breath or word from the mouth of Christ. With all of his great power the devil is defeated as if blown away by a whisper, by a puff of air from his nemesis. Lucifer, the light-bearer is sent into outer darkness forever and his hopes of defeating God are brought to nothing, it is a knock-out punch. The murderer is murdered. The accuser is accused. The deceiver is deceived by his own pride, the repeated life-pattern which leads to his downfall as Eiron defeats the bully Alazon. This character trait of pride and humiliation is the only life story the devil has. First in heaven, then in Eden, then at Calvary, then at the end of the world and beyond.

I'm aware, at this point in my mad ramblings that I may have gone too far. The irony being that the spurious hypothesis of irony in the devil's life is not making the devil look stupid. It is making me look stupid. Because people really do become unemployed and people really do struggle to have children and the very last thing I want to do is to write anything which will cause anyone pain. Because if that happens, I will have been used by the devil and that would be bitterly ironic. To an extent, all human beings are used by both God and the devil in turns – Saint Peter was rebuked as being used by the devil for unknowingly saying something to prevent Christ completing his work on earth. And at other times Saint Peter being praised by Christ and being a great help to his cause. So, all I can say is that if I have gone too far here then I'm sorry – it is not my intention to be less than human or to be used by the devil in any way. But if you would indulge my madness and viewpoint for a moment I think you may be able to see why some powers would want to trip me up one way or the other, either now or later. But I should take responsibility for the things that I write. I believe in personal demons (as well as personal angels) and as such I'm a dying breed. This is a view which was popular before the enlightenment. And I'm still disturbed by the dark epiphany that there really are fallen angels so it is not my intention to disturb others.

Also, the fact is that the devil has not been defeated yet – all we have is a sign (the cross) that he will be defeated one day. As far as I understand it (and who really understands it?) that is the crux of Christianity – that the events of the cross and the resurrection show how God in human form loves us enough to die for us and that these signs within Christ's life story (his death and resurrection) are the signs that death, suffering and the whole shebang of negativity will one day be no more. Which will be relatively good news when it happens.

Let's change tack, as I've strayed back into the land of dogmatism and possibly into evangelism. If there were a newspaper or a popular news website which had two interviews in it, one interview with God and one with the devil, it is God who would make the front page. The devil would ordinarily make the front page, but most people are more interested in God. Our battles (or wars) tend to be with God. All thinking men and women know that the devil, compared to God, is a no-one.

Chapter 7 – Irony in God's life

I write this chapter, like the rest of this book, from my own worldview and learning. 'Yeah, obviously, and your weird beliefs' I hear you think. I believe that Christ is God. I believe that he is infinitely more powerful than the devil. I believe (on my good days) that God is loving and that he is aware of the things that he allows. I believe that he has a conscience. I believe that he created irony and that he understands exactly what is ironic and what is not ironic. I believe that most of the angels also understand irony as they are creative and artistic beings. And that there are more angels than demons.

As has often been said – 'The onus is on the believer to bring forward evidence for God'. So this is my faltering, stuttering evidence. All of my attempts to prove God are full of fault and that is because the life I live is unrehearsed. I don't have the luxury of behaving in any other way. I make mistakes as much as the next person. As I say, you don't have to believe any of this, I am simply attempting to state my thoughts, experience and life story as evidence in the courtroom of the literary world (which has its own prosecutors, ushers and judges).

To detail the irony in the life of God the Father is a difficult task because most of us do not know his story in heaven. Even in terms of story he is eternal so there are no discernible beginnings or endings. He also created stories and time (which stories need). He created the shifting from one event to another and perhaps a better book would be titled: 'Stories – evidence for God'. One day (if you believe any of the Bible story) he creates angels. One day he creates the earth. He creates the things around him in heaven. He is nothing if not imaginative. He then seems to sit back in heaven and appears, to an extent, to neglect his creation.

It's fairly basic Christian theology to intellectually state that God is in the image of Christ. Christ himself stated this explicitly. "Those who have seen me have seen the Father," So the capricious, nasty God of many people's imaginations needs to take this claim into account. That Christ's character is God's character. And when it comes to feeling that God is cruel and nasty, we need to also ask, was Christ cruel and nasty? Because there is no accurate Christian understanding of a God apart from one with the same character as that of Jesus Christ.

To detail the irony in the life of Christ is a different matter. Here we must be concerned with the major ironies and the first and foremost comforting fact...

That Christ was subject to the same ironies as we are. He was acted as an Eiron, using humility to defeat the proud. He was both cut by and wielded the sword of irony. In fact, that may be the only comfort for the human condition – that God has been subject to the same ironic laws that people have to endure. That Christ lived under Murphy's

Law too (or Sod's Law if you prefer). That he played by his own rules.

Read about the acts of Christ in the gospels (his life story being the good news message that Christians are supposed to share). He spoke like a lion and acted like a lamb. His acts were gentle – he healed, he loved and he cared for people. So the malevolent God of our imaginations and experience is not quite the same as the kind and loving character of Christ. There's a discrepancy. The cruel god we fear is nothing like this God. This god is benevolent.

Many scholars have already written about the many ironies that littered Christ's life on earth. It is hard to cover them all so I will be leaving many out. So let's look at Christ's life. Firstly there is the birth. The place name of his birth is Bethlehem, meaning 'House of Bread' (Christ would later describe his flesh as bread). He was born to a family who were not rich. The devil could not orchestrate this irony. That Christ was destined to lead and save the world but was born into the most humble situation possible in an occupied land. He was born as an outsider, despite being the centre of all true love. He was born poor and temporarily homeless despite being rich in many other ways. This is a deliberate ironic orchestration in order both to fulfil the prophecy that he would be born in Bethlehem and also because it appeals to God's sense of irony. He could have been born in a palace but that is somehow less pleasing to God. It is not as ironic. This irony has been orchestrated by God. Chosen by him.

And then there is his name, said to be given by an angel to Mary and Joseph. His name is Jesus or Yeshua (in Hebrew), meaning 'God saves'. A truism. He lives up to his name and it is, as we have seen before, these truisms which can act as a modern day irony in the same way that not living up to a name is also ironic.

The name from which Jesus comes from is the name of God – Yahweh or Jehovah in our own tongue. Jesus or Yeshua come from this name. Literally 'Jehovah saves'. So what is the meaning of the name Jehovah or Yahweh? It tends to be agreed that the name means, 'I am who I am'. It doesn't take a genius to realise that the name of God is similar to the statement: 'I exist'. What kind of name is that? Who is named 'I exist'? Could God be giving a false name? It's a weird name. The interesting thing is that it is also like an occupation or role. God likes it when people believe he exists. He is pleased with that. If you believe that Christ is God then you can see God's character in Christ's character.

Then, as a child, Jesus ran off. He ran off to the temple in Jerusalem. And the authorities there, the teachers and scribes embraced him, listening to him as he taught them (the teachers). They sit, enthralled at his feet and his child heart must have swelled at the acceptance of the establishment. A childhood acceptance which would be ironically contrasted when he grew up. But in that first temple visit, all was as it should be, in the same way as a child in Britain today would perhaps dream of being friends with a member of the royal family and getting invited to the palace. This was no phoney dream for Christ – the establishment accepted him, in this instance, when he was a child. Did that influence his hopes and dreams for the future or did he always know what would happen in the future? The subsequent rejection and crushed dream.

Let's look at his occupations. Firstly he was a carpenter. Then he became a Jewish preacher and teacher. He didn't so much lose his job as a carpenter as move on to a new role. If he had a LinkedIn page there are no known periods of unemployment on his CV. (Depending perhaps on the significance which you give to the role of preacher.)

How is this ironic? Firstly there is the much commented irony in the carpentry. That he would be working with wood and nails and that he would die by wood and nails. This subtle irony is often commented on and represented in art. Next that he was making or creating things. Perhaps it would have been more ironic if he worked with clay and was a potter, but there is still an element of irony that he created the earth and everything in it and that he had a creative and practical role up until the age of around 30. He made useful things. Again there is the nepotism. Joseph, his earthly father, passed on the family business to him. Nobody knows if Jesus took over his father's job or whether his earthly father died when he was young. They may have worked together. It's likely that Joseph taught Jesus how to work with wood and create chairs, tables, yolks etc. And when Christ talks of yolks later in his life he knows what he is talking about. The weight of yolks is known to him. It's presumed that he never made cross beams to be used by the Romans in crucifixion (having integrity and ethics), but he would have made beams and planks. So when he talked about beams or planks in the eye it is slightly ironic being as he would have worked with wooden beams.

And at the age of 30 he received his calling to become a rabbi. Ironically he had no professional training in this. He had not been taught by the great rabbis of his day. He had not spent time in the temple or under the scribes or Pharisees. He was seemingly self-taught. He had no official qualifications (and yet is more qualified than anyone else to do the job). And as a result he must enter ministry from a different angle. Barriers to entry in the job role were high. The Pharisees and Sadducees held a monopoly on professional standards, their membership fees being loyalty. The itinerant preachers were held in low esteem. The Jewish religious leaders thought them unqualified and went so far as to claim that God was not with those who did not take the correct academic pathway into the profession. The same professional pride which goes on in our own day would have taken place then. Jesus was not officially qualified. Jesus was an outsider. He was not part of the establishment.

Again there is irony. That this outsider should overthrow the establishment. Or the true establishment overthrowing the false. That the most established person on the planet should act as an outsider and rebel. Was this a kind of greed? To want both the kudos of being the outsider and the legitimacy of holding the true power? Today many established people want to look like rebels simply because it is cooler to be a rebel. Even some politicians are called rebels when they are very clearly part of the establishment. Is the same principle taking place here? No qualifications, he just went off and started preaching. And he did his job well enough. 'Jehovah saves', he saves people from illness and diseases and disability. He saved a woman from stoning. He saved people from the horrible infringement of privacy which demon possession is. And the authorities later taunted that he couldn't save himself, when he was dying on the cross.

He gathered 12 men around him, a bit like Robin Hood. And it was this one man, this small team who were given the task of saving the world. Not only of saving some individuals but of defeating all evil and ultimately of defeating death. Of conquering the world. At least in his own life. And that one man's defeat of death is supposed to be a sign to us all of things to come.

Today, obviously, we do not see death defeated. We only read of one man who may or may not have defeated death once (as a sign). And we either believe that or not.

The only irony here is that the name seems not to be true. 'God saves' seems to be as ironic as it can be and not a truism at all. God doesn't save. We live, we die, our friends and family die. Illnesses are not healed. Death is not defeated. Even the common cold is not defeated. The devil appears to reign and the irony of the name of Christ seems to be too keen, too much like a sting itself. King of what? King of the deluded? King of the mad.

Further to this, he used irony within his parables and sayings. He went beyond peirastic (or 'testing') irony (although he used this on occasion with individuals when he was simply testing their faith). He used irony in parable – for example, in confronting the religious leaders of Israel in the parable of the tenants and the vineyard. Here his parable was effectively an allegory designed as a challenge. Or the parable of Dives and Lazarus (where he represents Abraham as saying to the rich man in Hades: 'If they will not listen to Moses and the Prophets, they would not be convinced even if somebody were to rise from the dead'). It's ironic because this is exactly what the gospels say happened to Christ (and Christians believe that he knew this when telling the story). As an aside, he also uses the name of one of his friends (Lazarus) as the hero of this story. Many of his parables use irony, from the Good Samaritan, through to the Prodigal Son. Or the rich man who saves up money and possessions all his life, intending to store them and enjoy his retirement, only to be told he will die the next day. Have a look at some of these parables in the Bible – they are rich in irony.

Christ also used immense irony in his sayings – the paradoxes he spoke about were often ironic in nature. And it's important to look at these.

And yet Christ was subject to irony. This is the crux of his whole life story. That he was also subject to Murphy's Law. If you want me to put it plainly – Christ got Sod's Law in the same way as we do. That is what makes this God different from so many others. The other gods seem to sit and smile in their heavens, but not Christ. He did not remain aloof.

Let's go back to his birth to show how he was subject to Murphy's Law. Anyone who has been made to wait in a queue which shouldn't be there will understand the Murphy's Law implications of this example. For you and me a queue is usually just an inconvenience. Unless we are engaged on an important task or face a deadline (a train or some other important meeting). In that case the people in a queue take on whole new attributes and the waiting seems designed to frustrate our plans. Those who require health care will also be familiar with queues and this is an area in which it seems that other people's needs often usurp our own.

Mary and Joseph had to travel to Bethlehem because the authorities required them to be there. Mary was heavily pregnant and after a long journey could have hoped for some kind of help in giving birth. Especially from God. No. All of the accommodation was taken. Other people with other needs had got in their first. People can be over-competitive and they had asserted their right to a good night's sleep in the Bethlehem inns. No room for the really important things. Except that this one family needed an inn more than any other family. This one family were on a very important mission which people say was the mission which would save the world. Saving the world, it appears, is no excuse when it comes to Murphy's Law and all of the rooms were taken. Imagine Joseph and Mary's frustration at this. Too many people. And they were at the back of the queue. What kind of Ironist would orchestrate this?

And later, in Christ's life, even the people of his own town and his own brothers and sisters don't believe in him. His own people rejected him.

Many people remark on the irony of Christ's death from torture on a cross. That he was a carpenter, and that he was so humbled. That he felt such pressure that his sweat was blood in the Garden of Gethsemane (a name meaning garden of the oil press). Dying at Golgotha (meaning place of a skull or skull-pan). And the irony that so few people see the love in that one battle faced by one man. He had even been so bold as to state that people would say, 'Physician, heal yourself' to him, only to have people taunt him on the cross, 'You who saved others, save yourself'. But out of weakness comes strength. And a love which is more powerful than death which can reverse ironies (or at least make iron when life hands out irony). Then there was he crown of thorns and the robe of royal purple colours they clothed him in. And Pilate writing 'INRI' – Jesus the Nazarene - King of the Jews.

Christ is an example of both an Eiron and an Alazon. He is both subject to and causing ironies. So did he create irony too? Being subject to the irony of fate hardly proves that you created it. Few people would suggest that the irony of Christ's birth in a stable was not orchestrated by God. It could be said that the crucifixion was the fault of the devil but there is another power overseeing the whole event. So, if Christ's life is an example then it would seem that some ironies are manipulated by the devil. Some by life. Some by people. And some by God. What could be said is that ironies can be turned around or redeemed. The cross is usually no longer seen as entirely tragic. The resurrection is irony defeated. The resurrection is God's irony.

Christ is a unique case in that he was not blind to the future or to the workings of irony. So when he told the parable of Dives and Lazarus and stated that people would not believe even if someone rose from the dead, the irony is lessened on himself because he is aware of the resurrection to come. The irony is on the listeners who include you and me. And this, again, is the nature of irony. It makes fools of the proud and humbles those who think they know it all.

From this, it seems that it is Christ or God and not the devil who is orchestrating some ironies.

Perhaps all that can be concluded is that God does orchestrate some ironies in our lives. But perhaps there is still hope that negative ironies can be turned into positive things in the same way that some suffering can. But cosmic irony, like fate, can even take place when an individual is proactively trying to turn an irony around. Sometimes it is the free will action which brings about the irony as a kind of self-fulfilling prophecy. But not always. It suggests that someone out there understands irony.

How did the writers of the gospels know that Christ had faced his own nemesis in the desert wilderness? How did they know that he had gone down into Hades after he himself had died and risen to life again? At some point it is Christ who has to explain things.

The thing about irony is that people do not always like it explained to them. It is like a joke which loses its force in the explaining. But for those of us who are slow (I speak for myself) it is important to explain some ironies. Sometimes we miss them and that is the greatest irony of all.

If you believe in some kind of God then you must admit that we are his creation – whether that is through evolution (which has its own narrative) or through some kind of creation (not necessarily a literal six day creation). In the same way that Dr Frankenstein created life, we too have been created. But monstrous or not, the creation is locked in a war with its 'master'. Dr Frankenstein's hubris was believing that he could create life and that everything would be wonderful as a result.

And maybe that was God's hubris too. God may not be as proud as Victor Frankenstein was, but in some ways his creation has turned on him and we are locked in a battle (which can only end in an icy wilderness for some of us). We blame God for the ironies. The devil is just a convenient character who sometimes seems only to exist to make God look better. God allows the ironies, whatever their source. And that appears to be negligence. Like the negligence of allowing excessive suffering. Of allowing Auschwitz or the Great Fire of London and plagues, or the modern-day concentration camps of North Korea. And it isn't just an appearance of negligence – it is an appearance of cruelty, a kind of micro-management into the affairs of individuals.

Of course, negligence and that level of cruelty are incompatible. You can't be absent and also a disciplinarian at the same time – but that is exactly how it appears. With God, it seems, when it comes to getting at us, nothing is impossible. It's a miracle in reverse which is impossible to prove and hard to express in conversation without appearing unhinged.

Chapter 8 – The Law of Irony

Religion can mess you up. Christianity included. But Christ can make things better. Nobody really knows what happens when you die. A lot of people seem to be born believing in a God and they carry this belief throughout their lives. Others struggle with the idea of any kind of God. Others are inclined not to believe. Those who do believe, instinctively, in God are often doubtful of his benevolence because of the arbitrary and fickle aspects of life. In a way, children are a lot more straightforward and will often arrive at beliefs and conclusions which are good enough but which get pummelled out of them by life and its sermons. Life is not a fair teacher and it is not a very good teacher. We can learn some things through pain and suffering, but we resent the teacher for it. We learn that life has favourites and it seems to expect a kind of worship which does not belong to it. That it is not entirely competent. (I know, I know, hubris.)

Hindu leaders and teachers have used karma as an evidence for God. The Vedanta and Nyaya schools state that the law of karma is evidence for the existence of God. That actions result in rewards and punishments but that karma itself has no intelligence in and of itself, that it is simply a law. Sankara suggests that someone must be controlling the law of karma.

There is less proof for the existence of karma than the existence of irony. Many people do not believe that synchronicities are coincidences and accidents. Irony has been proved. Or at least that we are formed in a way as to understand ironic instances. But like faith which allows some people to see the invisible, not everyone sees the irony. It is invisible. Like love. It is insulting to suggest that there is no such a thing as irony. And it is intellectually insulting to say that the narratives which we observe in our lives are entirely meaningless. It isn't just relativism, personal events can be seen by others. And, I would claim, by a higher power.

Karma is a spiritual law and Christianity also holds to spiritual laws. Specifically the laws that Christ taught through both his parables and his sayings. These sayings amount to paradoxes and there is irony in the real-life unfolding of a paradox. And here are some of the ironic sayings:

That if you give you will eventually receive.

That if you are proud you will eventually be humbled. And vice versa.

That if you seek and you shall often find.

That if you ask it shall often be given.

I'm adding to the original sayings of Christ by using the words 'eventually' and 'often'. That is because it is quite obvious that the humble are not always honoured in this lifetime. The proud are not always humbled. Sometimes they are in this lifetime, sometimes not.

But making up new spiritual laws doesn't really make sense, no matter how many Christian leaders believe that they have located a new law. For example, I heard one sermon in which the preacher asserted that God could not bless you past your last act of disobedience.

His new law would have been:
'If you are disobedient you will not be blessed by God until you become obedient again.'

But Christ never said that. It is plainly false, because if it were true, no-one would ever become a Christian.
The preacher had basically made it up. And he isn't the only one to do that. From preachers through to self-help gurus, people come up with fine sounding sayings and paradoxes. For example, M. Scott Peck says in *The Road Less Travelled*:

"The only real security in life lies in relishing life's insecurity."

That may have a kernel of truth and comfort in that, but most people know that it is not always the case. Sometimes security is not found in embracing insecurity.

Christ's laws are not made up. The strange fact is that he was either observing the way things are or else he created the spiritual laws, including the ironic aspects of these laws. Because the only laws of irony are the ones that Christ spoke of. At the very least, this proved that people 2000 years ago went through similar things to us. But Christ can even bypass his spiritual laws for us and that is because the law of love is greater than all. That nothing is impossible with God. This is known as grace. Throw all the laws out of the window and show mercy.

Was he simply observing? Was he cursing people when he said that those who judge will be judged or the measure we use will be used against us? These are ironies and paradoxes. Like the paradox of not getting stung if you grasp a nettle - which, incidentally, doesn't always work. But maybe that is the nature of a paradox – the exception proves the rule. That pride is punished and that humility is rewarded (because there are some good ironies). Some ironies are caused by God. And as I've written, I can't psychologically accept that God causes negative ironies. It does not compute in me. If he does then I would be very, very saddened by him. I would suggest that the war with God is justified and call for the whole of humanity to withhold love and praise towards God until he had learned his lesson. But there is an element of 'pride before a fall' of writing such things, like Sylvia Plath writing, "Dying is an art, like everything else. I do it exceptionally well." And then not dying particularly well. I'm being a bit disingenuous here as Plath was an excellent poet who died tragically and she was unlikely to be using her own authorial voice in the poem *Lady Lazarus*. But I'm trying to illustrate my theory and the pattern is that of excessive pride before a fall (eventually).

Anyway, as for me, I'm far too intelligent to die.

I hope your sense of irony is improving as you read this book (although it may be in spite of rather than because of these words).

Or take the saying, 'If you always do what you've always done, you always get what you've always got.' It doesn't always work that way. Sometimes it is a bit more complicated than that. Or take the law of attraction from the book *The Secret*. This involves visualisation, asking the universe and believing for something to come into your life (and the implication that negative thinking brings bad things into your life). Effectively it implies that a lack of self-control in thought is the only thing stopping you from getting what you want. But, let's be honest, so does religion – hence the irony, 'The pot calling the kettle black'.

There is only a law of irony insomuch as it is allowed by God. And that means that God is either negligent, permissive or inactive in the face of suffering. It is not a problem which can be solved. God allows suffering and he allows ironies to take place. And just as the devil is not the narrator of all suffering, he cannot be the narrator of all irony (including self-fulfilling or self-inflicted ironies).

So, in a nutshell, here is my claim. Irony is a fact. Irony suggests the presence of an intelligent, powerful force outside of ourselves. The nature of most irony is negative, therefore it hints at a malevolent power. And the presence of this negative power naturally implies the presence of a positive power. Or else the world is simply 'a tale told by an idiot, full of sound and fury, signifying nothing'.

I don't say it is proof. I suggest that it is evidence which is missed out, even though it is commonly and frequently experienced by the majority of humanity.

It is like the evidence given through longing, through thirst and hunger. That there is a need implies that there is a way of satisfying that need. And in all the other evidences for God – that there is a creation, so there must be a Creator. That there is a story so there must be a Storyteller. And in the same way, that there is an irony, that there is an Ironist. If there is no Ironist, if it is just chance and accident, then why is there serendipity or God-incidence? And why is negative irony so brutal and stinging? The patterns are there. Why would we evolve to see the patterns of irony? Seeing them doesn't help us to survive – on the contrary, it makes things worse. It makes people want to give up.

Take the hypothetical philosophy professor who is so intelligent that he can solve all of the deepest problems of mankind – he can explain every school of thought and theory when it comes to suffering and the meaning of life – and yet he can't seem to avoid suffering or find personal meaning. Despite his great intellect he falls into a deep depression, causing him to drink and lose his job and family. The irony of his situation isn't lost on him, but if he had not seen that irony he may have hoped for better things, but the irony causes him to sink into a deep despair and who knows where he ends up.

Why would an understanding of irony, a 'kicking a man while he is down' help anyone to survive? But what if an understanding of irony was placed there to hint at the existence of an Ironist? An Ironist who said: 'Whoever wants to save their life will lose it, but whoever loses their life for me will find it.'

Chapter 9 – The Creation of Irony

I woke up this morning to hear Alanis Morissette's song *'Ironic'* playing on the radio. It was the first song I heard. Was it irony or coincidence? Was it accident? After all, not all ironies are going to come from supernatural sources. Some ironies are just bad luck. Some ironies could simply be said to be a result of the fall of Adam and Eve, in the same way that Murphy's Law is a result of this. It is madness and simplistic to say it is always either God or the devil. Sometimes stuff happens and we interpret it in the way we interpret it. Sometimes irony is only in the eye of the beholder. But not always.

I would prefer to think it was a sign that God is moderately happy with me considering the circumstances. Such signs would not necessarily be an affirmation of everything I do (or write). After all, the worst kind of dogmatism is the person who claims that God agrees with everything he or she says and believes and then goes out to bully and brow-beat someone, all the time claiming that they are acting or speaking for God. That's what politicians do – their subtext is always that God is with them in every single opinion they have.

But some DJ on the local radio station playing *'Ironic'* would be an expression of love and meant as an encouragement to keep writing. Despite the many problems and distractions I have faced in this task. Many Christians live by signs like this – they are positive experiences and taken as expressions of love from God. Known in the Christian community as 'God-incidences'. But what if a song which plays on the radio is like vinegar to a wound? Maybe it is the timing, maybe it is the subject of the song or the memory it provokes. Why doesn't God get the blame for that if he gets the praise for a good irony? It's a valid question. The mental gymnastics of having God only responsible for good things and not bad things can simply be a sign of not wanting to displease God. As the scriptures say, 'Everyone wants to please their commanding officer'. I don't usually believe that God is the cause of bad ironies, but I suppose I would say that wouldn't I? If he really is responsible for bad ironies then he has some explaining to do.

But back to the song 'God-incidence'. This phenomenon, is sometimes known among left brain thinkers as confirmation bias – the tendency to search for information which acts as evidence for a belief (as someone once said, 'Seek and you shall find'). In life narrative there is a similar phenomenon in which an individual will assign significance and meaning to particular events which relate to their present circumstances. For example, as a Christian, I would naturally find meaning in all of those events in my life in which I have spoken or listened to people about God.

As a writer I ascribe significance to those important events which relate to writing. We are created to seek out evidence, order and pattern. We are also created to seek out meaning.

Back to the mundane ironies, those everyday ironies which can cause such trouble. Today the Met Office said there was a 70% chance of rain. In my 'glamourous' life I thought it would get me out of having to mow the lawn (a task I don't enjoy), but it simply wouldn't rain. It seems to rain all the time when I don't want it to rain, but as soon as I want it to rain it doesn't. (I can be self-centred at times.) So I mowed the lawn. As soon as I packed away the lawnmower it began to rain. Why wasn't God to blame for that? I'm using these trite example and aware that there are much more serious things.

Those who hang out washing experience similar incidents. These are mundane ironies and they are common. They litter the time between the major ironies which take place. Most thinking people will notice them. You can't blame the devil for things like that. How can you blame the devil for the weather unless you blame him for global warming? How can you blame the devil for natural disasters? You can't. But can you blame God? How is a volcano killing people an act like that of the acts of Christ? It is nothing like it. That kind of destruction is not an act of God. It is much more Godly to help in those circumstances. It is as if God is playing with humans at times like that. And when you try to use Murphy's Law to turn lemons into lemonade you find that a further irony prevents even that.

Do a quick search online of books called 'Don't Blame God'. There are lots of them. The best that could be said of them is that they conclude that it isn't wise to blame God. It isn't good for survival. But many of us blame him anyway. Blaming God is an act of base faith. It isn't great faith, but it is faith. You blame someone you believe may exist. And he loves us even when we are blaming him. We know that this is true because Christ loved those who blamed him.

So, back to the trite example. I can want it to rain and then decide to hang out washing as a kind of test only to find that irony personified seems to know my 'evil plan' and the sky remains stubbornly cloud free and the sun seems to have a lopsided smile. It is as if irony knows what you want because there is a personal force behind it which understands your plan. It all points to a personal opponent. It is, of course, highly egotistical – but human beings have egos (and so does God), the main place from which we view the world is from our own shoes. The world may not revolve around us, but some days it feels as if it does.

Even if you think that it is all chance and coincidence, you would have to admit that it very much seems as if there is a personal antagonist out to get us or playing with us as if we are toys. What kind of lessons are we supposed to learn from this except that the teacher has his favourites and we are not among them? That the teaching of life is not designed to allow growth and learning but pain and grief. That the teacher seems not to like us.

Moving on (swiftly) from this there is something called 'Apophenia'. Apophenia is the way in which certain patterns are found in random and often meaningless events. For example, the Twin Towers may fall down on 9/11 and part of the debris may form what is generally accepted to be the shape of a cross. But have someone who can see faces in clouds, trees and the wings of a butterfly and the excessively logical will say you have apophenia – clearly another evolutionary survival mechanism gone wrong (or, if you embrace social Darwinism, maybe it has gone very right and so the imaginative struggle to survive while the aggressively logical thrive). There are many other psychological phenomenon which can influence the mind or soul. Too many to go into here.

So, to the doubter and the cynic (and sometimes it is wise to be both of those things), hearing Alanis Morissette's *Ironic* while writing this book is not a sign. God is not giving me encouragement. God is not supplying material for this book. They still say, 'God is dead'. It is simply Alanis Morissette's popular song. And irony is not coincidence or bad luck anyway. Accidents are part of life and patterns are part of evolutionary survival. And irony is not bad luck.

Still, many people like to feel that God is somehow sending signs to say that he is reasonably happy with us. We are created to hope that God is with us to an extent, at least when we do the right things. That is human enough.

As I mentioned, in parts of the Christian community these kind of synchronicities are known as 'God-incidences'. God-incidences usually relate to positive meetings and ironies. They are basically a Christian version of serendipity. Serendipity implies that fortunate events or fortunate meetings and discoveries are based on chance. But it also hints at some kind of goodwill from the universe, some kind of power which puts a kind of blessing in the hands of an individual. God-incidences are explicitly stated as being blessings from God, so the element of chance is removed.

For example, two men may meet and get talking and find out that they hold information which can help each other. This is seen as a God-incidence. Or else a rainbow or butterfly or even a white feather may appear and act as a kind of comfort or a sign of God's comfort in an individual's life, perhaps following a grief or emotional upheaval. (We all face these griefs again and how are we to prepare for them?) This is closer to the kind of irony that God uses in that it can be a positive irony. Believing that God only uses good irony is based on his acts on earth as Christ – in which he only did good.

There is such a thing as a positive irony even though traditionally irony is linked to tragedy. Irony can also be linked to comedy, both in literature and in life. It is not always negative. For example, a friend of mine is unable to be frightened by horror films or scary TV scenes. He has watched the goriest, scariest films and TV programmes there are. Anyone who has watched some of the extremes of horror knows that as a genre, horror can be both frightening and gross, and the antagonists can be scary. But, for my friend, there is only one character on film or TV who can scare him - Bertie Bassett. Maybe this is not humorously ironic at all to my friend. But it is a relatively gentle irony.

To claim that positive irony comes from God and negative irony comes from the devil is simplistic and intellectually insulting too (and I certainly don't mean to do that). But I think there is an element of truth in the idea, even if it is a little more complicated than this. The trouble with stating that blessings come from God and negative events come from the devil is that life clearly attempts to teach us that this is not the case. God seems to be very much behind many of the negative things which happen, whether he simply allows them or orchestrates them. But once again we enter the endless cycle of trying to find rhyme or reason to suffering and there are no platitudes which are intellectually or emotionally satisfying enough to explain why bad things take place in our lives. But at least let's admit that some things are bad and some things are good and that it is inhuman not to apply this core value judgement. Sickness and death are not neutral things. They are bad.

But to be sure of the way in which God uses irony we need to look at the kind of irony that Christ used. And, in all honesty, his spoken irony was not always benevolent and kind. He spoke like a lion. Sometimes it seemed designed to crush the ego.

The spiritual laws which he created (or observed) humble the proud.

Woe to those who laugh now for they will cry.

Whoever wants to save his life will lose it.

Whoever lifts himself up will be humbled.

The first will be last.

These are not the characteristics of an entirely benevolent God as we would hope him to be. These are the characteristics of a God who applies moralistic value judgments and sets in motion all kinds of ways of separating the wheat from the chaff. Presumably, at the last judgment there will be irony aplenty. So why call the gospel the 'good news'? Is it to rub salt into the wounds? There is a hell? There is a second death? There is a devil? This is not good news at all. The gospel is only good news if your life is not going well. But the gospel is what it is (Incidentally, the 'whole gospel' is the life story of Christ).

To the atheist these things tend to hold no meaning. But to the believer, the sensitive or the right-brained thinker these things are signs. It is not feeble-mindedness which is the problem. The 'butterfly mind' of the imagination is another way of thinking. To an extent it is like another sense.

Above all, I do not want to lose you in this short book. It would be a further cruel irony to be misunderstood or to be obscure or esoteric. Or worse, to say something so inhuman as to cause suffering. That is not my intention. My responsibility is to try to explain what I mean as best I can in as human a way as possible in the time I have.

Inexplicable meetings can often be found both in real life and in soap operas. In soap operas 'Murphy's Law' rules. So, for example, a man may have a long-term girlfriend but in a moment of passion may kiss another woman in the soap. Nine times out of ten the girlfriend will walk in on this scene. Real life may be far less contrived than a soap opera, but there are elements of this kind of orchestration which really do occur. The soap opera mirrors the real life which we experience. It is a kind of distilled version of real life.

What I am attempting (perhaps badly) to argue is that these incidents, whether positive or negative, are orchestrated (or allowed) by a greater power almost in the same way as a soap opera is orchestrated by the writers and allowed by the producer.

I am not saying there is no free-will or that the actors in life cannot be proactive. I am simply saying that there are often higher forces which orchestrate some unavoidable events. The irony of fate. Irony is wielded by people, by God, by the devil (and presumably by angels and demons as delegated powers), and also by accident. Some ironies are accidents. Not everything is ironic.

Sometimes the irony is just bad luck. But who created luck?

For those of us who have been in this world for a while, we are aware that many ironic events will be negative. There is a value judgment which can be placed on an individual dying, losing a job, or an illness occurring. It is inhuman to suggest otherwise. These are bad things and most people will agree with that. We see these things in terms of narrative, in terms of story within our life stories. We give words and phrases to periods of our lives, even when they seem meaningless we may say, 'During that time everything was meaningless to me – it was like chaos'. And in this way we order and compartmentalise chapters of our lives. When we feel so lost that we have fallen out of any understandable plot-line for our lives, we may simply say we were lost or we had 'fallen out of our life stories'. We give names for things. We make names up for things. Academics make money and earn prestige out of naming things. It is a way of ordering the chaos. Hence we have strange books like this one.

So, in an attempt to order this haphazard reasoning I will go back to the basic hypothesis. That the ironies which happen within our lives point to the existence of God. And it isn't only humans who understand irony.

At this point you will notice that much of this writing still reads as gobbledegook. I would like to blame irony for this. Irony makes fools of those who try to analyse it. You can't pin down a butterfly and keep its beauty. If you've managed to read this far without throwing the book aside in frustration or anger then thank you. Although maybe it would be ironic to burn the book, absolutely hate it or leave a scathing one star review. Because this would be an example of character-based or character orchestrated irony. There is something within us which makes us want to use irony ourselves. We can't resist.

The nature of the ironies which take place are usually negative. I'm trying to use my own life as an example, for clarity, but perhaps it would make sense to look at the lives of others. Because clarity feels as far from me as the dark side of the moon.

Whereas God orchestrates miracles, the devil orchestrates seemingly supernatural cruelties and suffering. I call these things 'Elcarims' – literally miracles in reverse. If I were an academic I would perhaps earn a great deal of money for the idea and the naming of the word. As I'm an obscure writer it will have to be between you and I. Call them what you will, but for things to go so wrong in such an intricately manipulative way, leading people to cry: 'What are the chances of that!?!' then there has to be a negative force orchestrating events. The trouble being that a contrivance of a universe into making things go impossibly wrong is difficult to prove. In fact, attempting to prove it will just make you or I look silly (and of course, that is what a malevolent ironist would want). Miracles may be hard to prove, but so are Elcarims. How do you prove that events which seem to have no natural source really have been contrived by some outward force? How do you prove that Murphy's Law exists and that some force out there is making it happen? While attempting to do so you will either be laughed at or some life event will 'just happen' to snap you back to the less philosophical world of pressing need.

And, even if there is some personal ironist, why should this force necessarily be the devil of the Bible and not some other negative chaotic force? How is irony evidence for the Christian God? Or how is it not simply evidence for an evolved understanding of irony within human beings? My answer is that the life of Christ proves that he uses (and was subject to) irony. That the irony he talked about always eventually happens unless he rules otherwise. That pride comes before a fall. Each act of hubris has its nemesis. Icarus always flies too close to the sun. In the gospels Christ outlined the main laws of irony. He had either observed them happening and felt a need to comment on them – or else he was so familiar with them that it was almost as if he had set them into motion.

If irony were a side-effect of evolution then who would be better equipped to survive? Would it be those who understand irony or those who don't? I would suggest that you would survive a lot better (and probably even thrive) if you don't understand irony. There is no vinegar for a wound to those who don't understand irony. They dance through life. I'm assuming you're not thriving, but I have an ironic habit of being subjective when it comes to looking at other people. I often think everyone feels the same way about certain things and I think much of this book reveals that subjectivity. Maybe everyone in the world except for me is thriving. But it is hard to thrive when you understand irony.

Greek mythology also contained irony. These gods were fickle and capricious too. Challenge a god like Poseidon and he is going to make your life miserable if you ever dare to travel by sea. Have a pop at the devil and you may suffer for it. Tell Aphrodite that she is ugly and you may lose your looks. The irony of God may be as bitter, but at least it is tempered by love. Life would be intolerable if it were not tempered by love.

Chapter 10 – Who's to Blame?

Voltaire was a master of irony. Writing *Candide* and other biting satires he was wielding irony like a magic sword. Anyone who opposed him would feel the full force of his intellect and soon be reduced to smithereens in argument. He proudly declared '100 years from now Christianity will be dead'. 100 years later the place he penned those words had become a print house for Bibles. Some people dispute this version of events, but it shows how we want there to be irony. It shows how irony can be used as a weapon in debate.

There is something about cruel irony which attracts a certain type of person. For example, many computer viruses will find their way onto a computer through dodgy anti-virus software. Scammers in particular are fond of claiming to be the opposite of what they are and there is a small irony in this which is chosen by the scammer acting as the ironist. But maybe this is more a lack of imagination than a love of irony, since irony points towards intelligence. There are ironic company logos and all kinds of deliberate uses of irony in business, media, academia and so on. Many ironies are formed and executed by individuals and big business, there is no getting round this. In fact this is the largely accepted view – that irony is a man-made construct which is used and applied by humans (for better or for worse).

The use of irony in debate is common. There is the Socratic irony which is often used in questions (e.g.

'I'm new to all this. I was just wondering what happens to people who don't believe in God after they die?'). Many people who are antagonistic towards Christianity will use all kinds of tactics to make believers look foolish and lose an argument. The most effective of these tactics (for both sides) is to use story as a weapon. Christ used story as a weapon in debate and he did this very deliberately. That is because stories are remembered and they are used by people who have something important to say. Take the following story which was used by someone in debate who wanted to attack Christians and challenge the teaching on hell.

I had a dream about what really happens when you die. The Christians, who have believed in God will go to heaven. And so will everyone else. Except, in heaven, the Christians will be packed together in a small tin hut where they will sing worship songs to God thanking him for bringing them to heaven.

The other people in heaven, the non-believers, free and happy outside the hut asked God, 'Who are the poor people trapped in that tiny, stifling tin hut?'

And God replied: 'That's all the born again Christians. They seem to like it in there.'

This is actually quite a clever story in which the traditional expectations are reversed. The believers are effectively in a kind of hell and the non-believers are much closer to God than anyone else. It doesn't really need dissecting, it is what it is. And it is effective.

So using irony on other people carries a level of responsibility. And that responsibility is not always accepted. Sometimes it is used as the weapon to serve a purpose. This can be just as cruel as any irony of fate. Using irony in debate or in literature is an important skill which should require responsibility and ethics.

Irony in other people's lives is sometimes pretty obvious to all except the most ironically challenged. But, like Voltaire it is probably not wise to be too proud of your understanding of irony. He who lives by this sword can die by this sword.

Alongside this is the idea of 'Monkey's Paw' prayers. *The Monkey's Paw* is a classic short ghost story written by W. W. Jacobs. In the story the character Mr White (no irony there) comes across a mysterious severed monkey's paw which he is told allows the owner three wishes. Listening to his son, Mr White wishes for £200 to pay a bill. The next day he hears that his son has been mangled in a machine at the factory in which he works. His son is dead but the factory gives him £200 compensation. And so on with the other wishes. It's a clever little tale which uses irony as a plot device.

Or, to be blunt, take the man who thinks it would be nice to pray the Janis Joplin Mercedes Benz lyric "Oh Lord, won't you buy me a Mercedes Benz?" only to find himself stuck in some difficult job he hates where he has to drive a rusty Mercedes Benz van up and down the country. It is this kind of irony which people fear and which people will blame God for. And it all seems so personal. Or, as another example, perhaps someone would pray 'God, make me famous', and ten years later, following some nasty incidents, their face would be plastered over the papers and internet as 'the most evil person in the country'. Who is to blame for stuff like that?

And it is this kind of irony, alongside the everyday Murphy's Law ironies and synchronicities which can drive a person quite doolally. I'm understating – negative ironies can drive a person mad. The existence of synchronicities is, for most people, an interesting and mysterious topic. You may be humming a song in your head and all of a sudden there is the song on TV. This is not a negative event for most people. But magnify that event a hundred times because of illness, make a human being feel that the coincidences are acts of conspiracy and you have material or evidence for the kind of paranoia which can drive people over the edge. And some people genuinely struggle with this – they genuinely struggle with those unfortunate coincidences which seem to fill life. Like the headquarters of the good and under supported mental health charity *Rethink* just happening to be located opposite the MI5 headquarters in London. It is enough to drive the sanest person doolally.

I'm sure it is just coincidence. But there can only be so many coincidences. And people do not experience negative irony without external ironists.

The patterns are not in the eye of the beholder. The patterns are there. Trying to find rhyme or reason in any of this is, in itself, not enough. The value of humanity seems to be devalued by negative irony. So people like me attempt to stand back and reason it out and yet reason seems lacking. It seems personal. Like someone is out to get us. We deal with it and survive under it as best we can. Or else we claim there is no God and wait for the world to return to some semblance of normality. Going loopy or doolally is the only sane response for any human being in these circumstances.

I'm not going to try too hard to defend God for *The Monkey's Paw* fear. The general idea of Christianity is that if anyone asks Christ for something (persistently) then he won't use this kind of ironic trickery. Christ explicitly states that if someone asks for something good he won't give them something bad instead, strangely using the examples of an egg and a snake (and you can guarantee, someone, somewhere, has asked God for a Faberge egg). So, no matter how fond church leaders may be of telling stories about men and women who ask for something only to receive it in a negative way, it isn't really the spirit of what Christ was getting at. It is a kind of 'Monkey's Paw' God, full of trickery and one-up-manship, perpetually using irony to humiliate men and women. Usually these church stories will end with: "God has a sense of humour." But it isn't very funny to ask for something and to receive it in a way which causes distress or suffering. And if God is really like that, is he worth worshipping? After all, he allows far too much already. If God is real and he is as malevolent as we fear then is that character worth worshipping, even if he has unlimited power (although we may be deferential to many people for the sake of survival, is it really necessary to defer to a higher power who seems to act like an ar*e?)

Throughout this book I have deliberately used a weaponry metaphor for irony because it can be so destructive. This is not always a bad thing but perhaps when other characters in the metanarrative of life use irony it should be used as a defence or a shield. It certainly shouldn't be used to bully or harm. But it is. We are too much subject to ironists to inflict too many ironies on others. Besides which, it makes us no better than the ironists who use us for their pleasure. Even the Greek gods were better than that in their ironic judgements on the mortals. Use irony ethically.

It still makes fools of us all. For example, there are the other ironic spiritual laws from Christ...

The first will be last and the last will be first.

Whoever wants to save his life will lose it, but whoever loses his life for the gospel will find it.

Happy are those who mourn for they will be comforted.

Woe to those who laugh because they will cry.

Like a kind of weird rollercoaster. Counterintuitive paradoxes influence so many things in both the natural world and the spiritual realm. And so many of them hold hands with irony. Life itself holds hands with irony.

It is enough to drive the sanest person to the edge of reason. Even nature shows these counterintuitive elements. Stroke a nettle and it stings. Grasp it and it doesn't. Well, supposedly, but there is never any reason to Murphy's Law and nettles may sting those who grab them as much as those who brush against them. (And there are never any dock leaves when you need them anyway.) Murphy's Law or even Sod's Law tend to be the usual end point conclusion of most people who live long enough. They say that most of us live lives of quiet desperation. Bitter experience proves that God must be antagonistic and allow or cause events which seem to be part of a great conspiracy against the individual. Who wouldn't turn to vinegar after living in a world which seems to deliberately set out to drive an individual insane? Sometimes it is as if God himself is trying to drive men and women insane. And perhaps there is some truth in that – if it comforts you in any way to think that way.

There is good cause for our turning to vinegar, into moaning whinging complainers. Life is fickle and ironies are all around. We are the brunt of lessons and tests which we know nothing about. There are barely any parameters to the learning experience. Test follows test follows test without respite. And those who say, 'Lessons will be repeated until they are learnt' seem to be right (although remember that they have just made up a new spiritual law). We make the same mistakes again and again. And we are stubborn with it. Of course I speak for myself. Irony is the vinegar in the wound which life causes. And only those who do not love do not get wounded. In the face of this, depression or melancholy seems the only rational recourse. May as well just be saddened by it all like the writer of Ecclesiastes who lamented that everything was meaningless before hope took him prisoner again.

Like a poisoned sword, irony will pierce the mind of those who see and understand it. What advantage is there in this? What can be gained from understanding irony except to feel the full pain of suffering? We are like prisoners never seeing the face of the jailer and banging our heads repeatedly against the prison walls and all the time blaming God for putting those walls there. And it is not easy to get revenge against God or any invisible thing.

Of course the above is an example of a lament but bring irony into the equation and any lament is called a whinge or a whine. That's why a modern day Voltaire would rip this argument to shreds and throw it out of court. 'This is not evidence!' There is no logic or reason behind it as there is no rhyme or reason to suffering. It signifies nothing. And we are not in a courtroom. Not yet anyway.

But an awareness of irony will make you more careful. Your understanding of ironies in your own life and in the lives of others will protect you from ironists who are keen to use this sword against you. Use irony as a defence. Be aware of it. Look for it in the larger things not just the Murphy's Law everyday soap opera ironies which we all must face. And for those who don't understand irony at all. Good for you. You will save yourself the sting in the wounding. But in so doing you will be less likely to see any possibility of meaning in life.

Irony points towards a hope in a meaning to life. The conviction that there is a meaning, rather than the actual meaning itself. And the meaning of your own life rather than some global meaning. It implies some kind of personal omniscient force. That if someone is out to get you, someone out there also loves you.

If it is allowed by God then it takes the same place as suffering. It cannot be given any meaning. Perhaps all it does is prove that God is as disappointing as many of us fear him to be. An unsatisfying God. Is there anything worse? But like listening to two songs at the same time, one a mad cry of someone who yields the sword of irony and the other a lullaby - there is another voice behind this. There is a soothing voice. A voice which comforts. The voice of the ironist and the voice of the one who has allowed (not caused) the irony to take place. His only crime is his apparent neglect, permissiveness or leniency in allowing the suffering.

Atheists will often debate this crime with great skill. It is the suffering argument and there are no satisfying answers. I don't think it will ever be resolved in this lifetime. There are only stories and sayings we tell ourselves to cope with life. Atheists will use the picture of the man who stands by and does nothing when he sees someone murder or rape the family of another man. Is the first man to blame? Only inasmuch as he does not act. Perhaps his heart goes out to the man who suffers the loss of his family. And so the atheists will say that if a man is responsible for allowing such things, how much more would a God be responsible for allowing things such as the Black Death and great fire of London, or our own personal plagues? There is no adequate answer to it and I will not attempt to provide one. It would be inhuman.

But who is really to blame? If there genuinely is an invisible ironist or ironists then is it God? How can Christ be subject to ironies from the devil? And if God is as good and loving as people keep saying he is then why would he allow (or cause) such biting ironies? I would conclude in literary terms. Irony can come from God, the Author, or at the very least be allowed by him. If God has a conscience then he must be willing to allow the Alazon (the subject of the irony) to reverse the irony. That is his responsibility and he shouldn't attempt to duck out of that by placing the responsibility back on humans. The dispute between humans and God is one of responsibility. And believers shouldn't attempt to keep God's reputation so pristine and clean at the expense of those who suffer. We all 'want to please our commanding officer', but at what cost? What pyrrhic victory against honesty? He can handle questions and even blame. He loves us even when we blame him. But most people act as both Eirons and Alazons (and it is better to be the Eiron).

Irony is more often used by the devil, the antagonist or else a result of the Fall - of the way life is. The proof of this is in the cruel nature of the irony. A number of spiritual ironies come from the laws which Christ brought into being. These specifically centre on the humbling of pride and all kinds of reversals and paradoxes. Effectively this is irony from the protagonist or hero. Irony can also come through the characters (such as Voltaire) or other individuals. And finally, irony can simply be a matter of the human condition. Sometimes these ironies are simply allowed by the Author and recognised by some of the characters.

Chapter 11 – Irony as Evidence for God

Well done on making it this far. Thank you.

Despite my best efforts I fear I haven't expressed what I meant as lucidly as I had hoped. I've been all over the shop. I've been at turns defensive, obscure and downright confusing. I also fear that I haven't been as pragmatic as I had hoped to be – there have been very few practical suggestions made – so I hope to redress that in the remains of this book (which, ironically, may remain unpublished).

It's a big ask. It's a big ask to expect you to believe that irony means that God exists. And then to go beyond that and ask you to believe that this God is good. That is ironic in itself (given the nature of most ironies). The man scraping his vehicle windscreen free of solid ice one cold winter morning can be at war with God for that moment, but to suggest that God causes irony too? That's just giving more ammunition to the man. So we swear and scrape the ice away from the windscreen and shake our fists at a God we may not really know. What kind of monster would subject humans to suffering anyway? What kind of sick, depraved mad God would do that?

I believe in God but I struggle to believe in a good God, although I guess this is the truth. I am half persuaded by life and experience that God is not benevolent, but I am longing for God to be better than that. To be the better person. A God not in my own image... as my own character is far more prone to over-reaction and mood swings (although not tyranny).

It's said that all mankind is at war with God and that becoming a Christian is a surrender in that war. That you either serve God or serve the devil. If nothing is impossible with God (as he says) then perhaps it is not as simple as that, maybe there really are a lot of objective people on the fence. Becoming a Christian is a truce, it is a cessation of animosity and hostilities. Sometimes fights flare up again but ideally the war is over (or there is some kind of workable deal).

So am I asking you to believe in a God I don't believe in myself? No, that would be an ironic hypocrisy. I do sometimes believe that God is love and that he is the source of all love. And I do usually believe that God has the same character traits as Christ. But when we are suffering it is hard to see even Christ as entirely good and merciful. What we see then is Christ angry at the Pharisees and Scribes. At Christ speaking sternly about hell and the necessity of forgiving. About Christ angrily turning tables in the temple or cursing a fig tree. Or any one of the harsh things he said. At least, we focus on these things if we have learned about them. The irony is that so few of us read our Bibles.

There is even irony in Christ's 'forgiveness law' of forgiving to be forgiven (and vice versa). Once again this is a sensitive issue as it is almost impossible to ask people to forgive. Few succeed anyway and forgiveness is more of a journey than a destination. And for those of us who do fail to forgive? Christ likens our state to that of prisoners with God as the jailer or head warden. He rules with an iron rod in this and what a bitter irony that is. To be the one to suffer for someone else's sin. That if we don't forgive people who have harshly wronged us that we (and not those who did the wrong) get punished? What kind of sick irony is that? Favouring the perpetrator over the victim. So metaphorical prisons become self-fulfilling prophecies because we get trapped in wanting revenge. There are all kinds of prisons, as has been said before (and let's try and not let that sentence become ironic).

How do we reconcile cruel irony with a good, kind, loving God? We don't. And it is no good to talk about a 'tension'. This is more than a 'tension'. We shake our fists at invisible walls and rant and curse against a God who seems to have his feet up in his office probably smoking a cigar, swigging ambrosia from a bottle singing, 'Dems de rules people'. Or else we give him the silent treatment. Or else we lose all hope in any kind of meaning in this life and become persuaded that there is no God.

And God has hardly made himself vulnerable in our lifetimes. He is well protected. I hope he will forgive me this other harsh accusation (and obviously, all the other inferred accusations - I want to please my commanding officer as much as the next man - but not at the expense of honesty).

So men and women are at warfare with God and it is understandable in many ways.

I overheard a woman talking to her friend when a street preacher told people that they needed to say sorry to God. "No," she said to her friend. "He needs to say sorry to me". Well, at least she believed in God. But I could sympathise as I'm often in the same place. God seems to be perpetually rooting for an apology and yet we feel as if we are the wronged party. And all those who side with God can feel like vinegar to our wounds. Quit defending God. He can do that himself. Don't keep him clean and pristine at the expense of love towards others. Or humanity.

The irony of our condition is that many of us feel that way. But the further irony is that those who humble themselves into an apology to God can begin some kind of meaningful dialogue. The humble are lifted up. Eventually.

I'm aware that this book is beginning to sound like an evangelical sermon and I never set out to write a sermon. I am not a leader, I am a writer and a human being and I'm simply trying to make sense of this world. Let me change my tack and get back to the theme and my point...

Where do these ironies really come from? If the perception of irony really was an evolutionary phenomenon then why do we perceive it? How does it aid life or survival?

My premise throughout this book is that the irony is evidence for an Ironist.

So the proud are humbled, so what? Was Christ simply commenting on the laws he saw at work? Or had he somehow set those laws in motion before he even spoke the words (as most Christians would believe)? And if he created laws of physics and every other kind of natural law, is the law of irony any different? And if it is no different then is he no more responsible for ironies than he is for gravity? And if he can stop the law of gravity by walking on water can he stop his other laws?

Orthodox evangelical Christianity would assent that God could be behind the ironies. Take, once again, the irony of humility. The humble are said to be honoured, the proud are said to be humbled and receive shame. The time scale for this law is unknown and it sounds like a kind of Christian karma. But is humbling people really a Godly thing to do? Or is it more Godly to give honour to the humble? And when the humble have been 'lifted up', is the cycle repeated if they become proud? Or if those who mourn are given laughter will they in turn mourn again as a kind of pattern? When we see people laughing have they always been crying some time before? And vice versa?

Woe to those who try to understand irony and paradox for they will be confused. Woe to those who make up fake spiritual laws.

If irony causes suffering, as a kind of vinegar to a wound, in what sense is that Godly? Is God to be seen only in the wind and the fire and never in the gentle whisper?

Yes, it is not intellectually satisfying to suggest that God is only in the good ironies. He also seems to be in the bad ironies. For here is the evidence - that we perceive the irony to take place, that we attach a value judgement to that irony, that it appears to be orchestrated. That we are thought mad for even believing that something or someone seems to be out to get us. That in attempting to communicate these feelings or express these things we are either unable to do so or else ridiculed for it. Or else we do not even see the ironies and are at least spared the sensation that suffering appears to come from God. For those who are concerned about survival, it is an intellectual luxury to even care about such things, like asking, 'What is the point or meaning of work and career?'

If you are in survival mode you don't really care about such things, you care about surviving. And if everyone who wants to save his life will lose it then why do we have such a strong survival instinct? What kind of God would implement such laws? And is God always willing such laws on or do they just happen as gravity does? So that he may not be the one willing a plane to fall from the sky, as it is simply gravity, laws which have been put in motion from the beginning. Is irony the same? If it is then it is no more evidence for God than gravity or any other law is. But do laws imply a Lawgiver? And more importantly, can they be bypassed? If nothing is impossible with God then why is he so bound by his own words? Christ said nothing is impossible with God – isn't that at least as important as the rest of the things he said? And aren't his actions gentler than his words? A lamb in actions and a lion in the way he speaks.

Because his actions, according to the gospel (his life story) were (and are) so loving, gentle and kind I would like to conclude that God is found only in the positive ironies. I know that this is simply an opinion but I find it the only position which makes sense. Clearly, psychologically, I find it the only position which I can accept in order to retain my tenuous link with sanity. If God is good then it isn't Godly to orchestrate negative ironies. Once again, my reasoning here (faulty as it may be) is that it is simply not Godly to inflict suffering (and irony can be linked with suffering). I'm aware that I'm repeating myself but I have more questions than answers.

So am I being simplistic or unduly sycophantic by suggesting that God only perpetrates the positive ironies? Not entirely. I take this position because it is the only position which makes sense to me. I can't see any aspect of God in pain, in suffering or in negative irony. I'm not suggesting that all negative irony comes from the devil. I'm suggesting that some does. But God can be seen in the love, in the care and in the positive ironies. Whatever the words of Christ, the actions of Christ prove this to be the character of God (if you can believe that Christ is God). Actions of healing and self-sacrifice, of care and compassion and kindness. In the gospels he was rarely angry and only because of the abuses and manipulations of the powerful. Therefore the negative ironies cannot be sourced in him.

This, I admit, sounds like the ultimate act of sycophancy, of someone who hopes to duck suffering by praising God. But it is not entirely that. It is that a God who causes suffering, who causes negative ironies is not worth worshipping. But if God is, in truth, a God who orchestrates all kinds of ways in which men and women can be humiliated and deconstructed then that is between God and his conscience. He has to take responsibility if that is the truth.

How then, is irony evidence for God? Even if it is evidence for a higher power, how is it evidence for a Christian God? Why isn't it evidence for one of the many other gods? Why isn't it evidence for ascended masters or for angels or for any number of powerful forces? Why isn't it evidence for an impersonal force? Why does it have to be evidence for the Judeo-Christian God?

Because the majority of the ironies follow the pattern of Christ's teachings:

The humble are often praised.

The proud are often humbled.

People who want to save their lives often lose them.

People who don't care about their lives often survive.

The laughing go on to cry.

The crying go on to laugh.

And most importantly, because Christ was the only God we have who was subject to these ironies and sufferings too.

My point is this: That irony, because of the nature of irony (and the need irony has for an audience) automatically points to an ironist. People don't just understand (or not understand) irony because brains have evolved that way. Like the parables of Christ, irony separates an audience between those who understand it and those who don't. That great writers such as Voltaire could use irony to crush the Christian faith was itself ironic because irony was originally made by Christ. It was ironic whether the Bible printing story is true or not. Christ using irony proves that sometimes God uses irony too. And in that there is a hint of meaning.

In the same way that a longing, a thirst or a hunger points to there being a way of satisfying that thirst or hunger, an irony points to an ironist. I am simply claiming that this ultimate Ironist is Christ. That Christ is God and that he made irony and continues to use irony.

If anything were to put a man or woman off faith then maybe it would be this very suggestion. But I am attempting to claim that there are other ironists and a God who causes cruel ironies is not worth worshipping. That it is not God-like to cause Christopher Reeve, Superman to lose the use of his legs. It is ironic, but it is not God-like. I'm suggesting that ironies like this are either accidents or caused by an antagonist to humanity. And that the existence of this antagonist hints at an existence of God. Accidental ironies can occur and with the confusion and chaos of life maybe it is to be expected. Accidents are said, by many Christians, to occur as a result of the Fall. People get ill, people are born, people die, sometimes we see patterns in their lives, sometimes tragedy happens.

And so I am claiming, as clearly as I can, that irony is evidence for God. And that the evidence for irony is found all around us.

But so what?

Who cares and so what?

If this were all true then wouldn't we all be subject to powers over which we have no control?

Chapter 12 – Irony in Your Life

If there were a newspaper or website devoted to your own life, what would be the recurring front page headline? And would you see the ironies in the stories? And would seeing them make things better in any meaningful way?

Indulge me as an intrusive narrator (and not entirely reliable) and take a moment to look at the ironies in your own life. These ironies will almost always be to do with occupations, roles, names, illnesses or major life choices. The nature of irony is such that it will make the wisest person appear a fool. Irony will not allow you to see every aspect of its working in your life. I have already personified irony as a pernicious entity or a violent weapon. It doesn't want you to see every aspect of its workings. The Johari window is said to be divided into four. One of these windows includes other people seeing ironies in your life which you cannot see. It is like seeing faces in trees or clouds, when the face is pointed out it is easy to see. But left to our own devices we don't necessarily see the pattern.

You will spot a number of ironies in this book. Like the famous Alanis song and like the equally famous comedy sketch which claims that none of the Alanis ironies are in fact ironies. In the same way, some of the ironies detailed in this book are debatable. But maybe, as I mentioned, all of Alanis Morissette's ironies are ironies but people can't see them. I'm calling for a wider definition to irony. I'm not saying that all of these ironies are traditionally accurate given a strict interpretation of the definition of irony. Irony makes a fool of anyone who attempts to wield this sword. And you don't use a sword in a boxing ring.

You should be aware of at least some ironies in your life. Being aware of these ironies will at least give you a greater insight into your life. Whether or not you consider these ironies to be the result of bad luck, coincidence or the meaningless human condition, I am simply asking you for a moment to consider that they are known to God. I am, remember, not saying that God has always caused the irony. I am simply suggesting that they are part of a narrative which isn't over yet. Your story isn't over and it is never too late. Clump the ironies into two sections - those which can be changed and those that cannot be changed. Deal with them like problems or puzzles to be solved. Make iron from the irony.

I'm aware that I have been talking about serious issues which affect everyone on this planet and irony is often linked with suffering. So please don't think that I have intended to deal with the issue crassly or glibly. I realise that many people do suffer intense, tragic and cruel ironies. That you will probably have faced bitter ironies. I am not trying to negate the validity of that suffering. I am not even attempting to find meaning in that suffering. I am simply claiming that there is a gentle and kind God who cares for humanity. Who sympathises with the human condition and who became subject to the same rules.

There would be no rhyme or reason to any irony if the one who created the law of irony did not make himself subject to that same law. And he did, in Christ Jesus. Any power which wields the sword of irony and is not subject to it is no kind of god of any worth. If Christ isn't God, he should be.

That is one story I offer to help you to cope. And I offer it because it helps me to cope. You may need a different story, but I may not hold that story. It may be that only God holds that story for you. But if that is the case then I would advise that you dialogue with the one who holds your whole life story in his hands. If you are unable or unwilling to talk with him right now, then at least think about doing so at some point. He is usually rooting for some kind of apology and we are deferential enough to apologise to those with power simply for the sake of survival in this world. Although, obviously, when it comes to apologising, God is not really practicing what he preaches and it would be nice to see him take the lead in that. (Sorry God, but it would.) Ah the irony.

Conclusion

While writing this book, the British swimmer Adam Peaty broke the world record and won gold in the Olympic 100m breaststroke in Rio. As a child he had a phobia of water. It would have been more ironic if he had been named Adam Waterman, or Adam Landy, but you can't have it all. Adam Peaty's win is an example of how irony can be used for good – how something can be transformed from a negative to a positive irony. And it's far more positive than America's first gold medal being in a shooting contest. When life gives you irony, try to make iron.

In writing a book about irony I'm leaving myself open to all kinds of possibilities (some of them possibly quite negative). Not least the possibility of being laughed at for some of the outrageous theories and certainly for attempting to bring forward new evidence for the existence of God. Or worse – not even being laughed at, just being ignored. It's like a strange rewriting of the Emperor's New Clothes – some people will always say there are no clothes and no king either. Invisible things are hard to prove in a materialistic culture. An invisible devil is, to an extent, out to get people like me (for which my defence is that I refuse to live this life without saying the blindingly obvious about the devil being a violent, hypocritical, bullying git (gulp)).

In this short book I have briefly attempted to cover some of the major ironies in the lives of Christ, the devil and my own life. In the process of doing this I have missed some huge ironies and that is, of course, itself comically ironic. Like Alanis Morissette – what is the point of writing about irony if you don't understand the definition in the first place? I have extended the definition of irony to Murphy's Law, hypocrisy, synchronicity, God-incidents and a whole host of the smaller ironies which people will often put down to bad luck. That this attempt turns to gobbledegook is a huge problem. That I have rambled is obvious. The irony could be that this book never sees the light of day. That it becomes known as one of the most deluded, unsound, spurious arguments ever made. That it is read by no-one. That people would consider it ironic to give it a very bad review because of the dodgy logic. I was not created as a logical man – that is my only defence there. I was created imaginative, not logical.

This is the nature of the force called irony. Attempting to comment on it is like trying to pin fire to a butterfly board or jar the wind. You can't do it. You just end up with feverish similes and no lasting lucid comments. That is why it has rarely been done before – at the very least you must admit that it is original. I have tried to make this book as accessible as possible. I understand that much of what I have stated may sound more like a rant or a whinge than a serious claim. This has been my first venture into non-fiction and although I have tried to use irony in the fiction which I have written I am not suggesting that this short book is an in depth view on this subject. It is flawed as I am, subject to the same laws of irony that we all are. But let's not anthropomorphise a book.

What I have claimed is that irony is evidence for the existence of God. It is not proof of the existence of God because, ironically, God does not want to be proved yet. There are a whole set of other evidences for the existence of God which you will find in many books. Books about creation. Books about philosophy and history and science. Books written with a lot more clarity than this one (but please forgive me that… I blame the devil). I hope that I have not strayed into outright insanity (but as I have noted, I may not be a reliable narrator).

I have come to the subject as a writer, author and journalist. I have chosen this particular theme because it is the main phenomenon which sustains my own faith.

In your own life you will almost certainly be aware of many ironies – and if you are not, maybe it's time to worry. Remember that the major ironies are to do with your name, your occupation, your birth, your health and your death – try to keep the mundane ironies and the little miracles in reverse, the 'elcarims' into perspective. They are annoying but most people seem to have to put up with them.

Pragmatically it is important to be aware that the cliché 'pride comes before a fall' holds far too much truth in it. In being aware of that it makes sense to attempt to avoid arrogance in the hope that one day there would be some kind of reward. I have not attempted to answer the suffering question because I don't think it can be resolved in this lifetime. All we have are stories that help us to cope, like stones in the mouth to simulate water while we are walking in a desert. So, when it comes to cruel ironies it is important to be as proactive as possible. Many cruel ironies can be overturned and they don't have to be permanent. If God has only allowed an irony then they don't always have to be put up with.

My claim is that these ironies are significant and that they are allowed and understood by God. They are understood because he has been subject to them as well. Hence he can sympathise (if he has a good memory). My claim is that many of these ironies are so bitter and so cruel that they are orchestrated. I am not claiming that they are orchestrated by God. But I am claiming that they are allowed by God. Knowing who is behind each irony is important. I would state that the most negative, cruel ironies are almost certainly not from God. As for the good ironies, the God-incidences, the serendipity – I claim that these are orchestrated by God because this kind of irony is more in keeping with the character of Christ.

The reason I claim a benevolent or good God is because it is a coping mechanism – I'm not too worried about defending him – if he really is as pernicious as many think then what can anyone do anyway? Why would expressing such a thought be offensive? Can't God take it? Maybe it is just a coping mechanism to want to believe that God is kind rather than cruel. He is the only real God we have got.

When a book of fiction is written there is often an author and a narrative voice. The narrator is not the author, but he or she seemingly possesses power. The author is usually one step away from the narrator. So an unreliable narrator may be malevolent, an anti-hero of a kind, but that doesn't mean that the author is. Antagonists aside, there are all kinds of other characters. My further claim is that as characters, we have a level of free will which can turn these ironies around. Life itself, may have the power to create bitter irony. But as characters who act under the tyranny of life we are able to make changes. The oft repeated phrase, 'When life gives you lemons, make lemonade' is only a cliché because it can be effective. When life gives you irony, make iron.

As you may have noticed, my logic has been suspect and I have walked a line between out and out madness and speculation. My defence is that it is the only way to approach this subject – it cannot be approached with logic alone. Reason is not always an adequate enough instrument to analyse the situation. Perhaps I have completely failed to pin down this fire or jar this wind – to describe this sword. Perhaps I have only succeeded in mixing unhelpful metaphors. Besides which, does it even have a beauty which could be captured?

I would prefer to end this book as hopefully as I can and with as much comfort as I can offer. The ironies which life makes can often be turned around. And that is because the Author, the source of good ironies is kind and merciful and the cruellest ironies don't come from him. It is possible to be proactive and to make sure that ironies which occur are transformed once they happen. Or, if they can't, that they are used in some productive way. Be as proactive as possible in response. Cruel ironies only hold true power if they are caused by God – and they are not, even though they may appear to be.

The ironists, the Eirons, do not always have to be the ones to act, we as characters get a say too – or else we can use irony ourselves for good purposes. As characters we can decide what we believe and we have choices in the way we act and respond to the things which happen to us. Although there are many things we cannot change, as Victor Frankl said, we still control the last freedom of being able to choose our attitude. And even if that is taken away there are other things we can do, other freedoms we can defend. By acting, by attempting to transform those negative ironies into something better we can become more proactive. Irony does not have to be fate. And we do not have to believe that a negative irony is from God.

I have used the semantics I have chosen in this book in the hope of analysing the situation as best I can. In no way am I implying that right and wrong are just relativistic accidents of an uncaring universe. Irony, as an accident of an uncaring universe is an unsatisfying conclusion to make. And although many people would say that this is the way things are and that it is part of the human condition, there are many problems with that conclusion. It is not an easy thing for a soul to embrace that conclusion. And that is the reason that it is so hard to accept – because, ironically, we have souls and a soul searches for meaning. This too is part of the human condition. (I know, I know, dogmatism…)

When it comes to meaning and irony we are in the same realm as that of meaning and suffering. As with suffering, irony can be intensely personal and intimate in its cruelty. So the phrase 'It's not personal' doesn't satisfy the individual. It is personal. In the pain of suffering it is as if God himself is causing these things, it is as if someone up there has got it in for us. It is very much as if that is the case. So what irony does, is to point towards evidence for the existence of God. A small life lesson which may not take away the suffering or the irony, but which can, at the least, hint at someone who can.

The root meaning of God's Old Testament name (Yahweh) has been translated as: 'I am who I am'. It is a strange name to have. Ironies often gravitate to names and in this case it seems that it doesn't exclude God's names. I'm not saying that irony is God. I'm saying that God has 'allowed' himself to be subject to ironies too. And this is the only genuine sop of comfort or answer to the problem I can offer. Because it is this which I find to be the only personal comfort in my own life when irony cuts like a sword.

As I have mentioned before, the only comfort I can offer is that Christ allowed himself to be subject to the same rules and laws which we face, including Murphy's Law and the law of irony. This is true of both irony and suffering which, as I have mentioned, are often linked. I also find it helpful to engage in dialogue with God (if only occasionally).

It is far more God-like to relieve suffering or to transform the cruellest ironies into something better.

People make mistakes and those of us who see irony find that it is like vinegar to a wound. Like the poison on the tip of a sword.

So what is the use then of seeing irony? Because it remains evidence that there is a power greater than irony and greater than life and that power is love. And more than that, it is a sign of intelligence. Pity the person who sees no irony anywhere (although, ironically, perhaps he or she could be the happiest person in the world).

Above all, love is stronger than irony and all the laws of irony. Ironies can be transformed because love is greater than life and all of the spiritual laws and Murphy's Laws which we are subject to. Love is stronger.

And they say that God is Love.

So, to conclude. Don't tempt the irony of fate. Try to avoid hubris. Don't name a ship 'The Invincible' and expect it to win battles. Don't name a ship 'The Titanic' and herald it as unsinkable. Don't call a rose 'Prosperity' and expect it to thrive. Be careful how you name your children (if you have any). And be careful what you say. But not too careful. To be careful of every thought we have and every word we utter would drain any joy left in life (and there is evidence enough for joy too). It isn't a matter of self-control of the brain or the tongue – that would be neo-puritanism or the kind of popular self-help advice which never really helps. It is better to avoid a persistent attitude of arrogance, not the occasional proud thought. I was humbled because I was arrogant, not because some stray thought entered my mind.

Obviously, excessive care would drain any fun left in life. Excessive care is no fun and most of us avoid hubris quite easily yet still stuffer. If irony searches our thoughts and hearts for pride then we may as well say things like, 'I'm too intelligent to die'. What the hell, say what you want, it's a free country. But be aware of these strange, wild and fickle powers that seem to delight in our sufferings.

The proud are eventually humbled but that means that the humble are lifted up in the end. If the first are last, it also means that the last will be first. Those who want to save their lives may lose them, but the unselfish are protected. (But still, why put such a great survival instinct within humans and animals?) These aren't simply paradoxes. They are ironies.

And if God has not put himself subject to the same irony as the rest of us, is he worth believing in? And if there is no God at all - why are there so many shapes in the clouds, trees and the butterfly wings?

Jesus told them, "It is not the healthy who need a doctor, but the sick. I have not come to call the righteous, but sinners."'

Mark 2:17

About the Author

Nick White is a professional writer who lives in the Midlands, UK.

Website: www.nickwhitewriting.com

Blog: Stories Make The World Go 'Round

Twitter: @nickcwhite

Printed in Great Britain
by Amazon